M

&

DAVID PEACOCK

AWARENESS

The Groundwork For Fulfillment

Hopefully we will
get to see more of you
at heats

Together we're
better

Tellwell Talent
www.tellwell.ca

ISBN
978-0-2288-0529-8 (Paperback)
978-0-2288-0530-4 (eBook)

TABLE OF CONTENTS

FOREWORD

BY BOB PROCTOR

I've read thousands of books over the past fifty-seven years. One of my favourites, *The Power of Awareness*, teaches us that all our results in life are an expression of our level of awareness. The more aware we are, the better our results.

In *Awareness: The Groundwork for Fulfillment*, David Peacock and Myles DeBrincat dive deeper into many of the timeless ideas presented in *The Power of Awareness*. If you grasp the concepts presented and discipline yourself to act on them, they have the power to change your life.

There are many gems to reap from this book; however, one thing really sticks out for me because it's not something you often hear or think about. David and Myles explain that you must raise both your level of awareness (your consciousness) and your "simple-awareness" to enjoy a far more rewarding and meaningful life. If you do the exercises and practice the techniques the authors suggest for developing both types of awareness, you will live in a state of "flowing fulfillment."

This book is full of valuable strategies and exercises to show you how to live with a feeling of inner contentment as you take actions that are aligned with your values and purpose. As you move through each chapter, you'll gain more and more insight into who you are, what makes you tick, and what gives your life meaning.

The ideas and practices presented in this book will require discipline and repetition to make them habits. However, I know from firsthand experience that expanding your level of awareness and doing new things that cause you to grow is always worth it.

Earl Nightingale said, *"The more intensely we feel about an idea or a goal, the more assuredly the idea, buried deep in our subconscious, will direct us along the path to its fulfillment."*

David and Myles will show you that although the journey to fulfillment is different for everyone, the feeling of fulfillment is similar for each of us. It's a feeling of inner contentment, inner peace, and the knowledge that you already have everything you truly want.

This book not only shows you how to create that feeling but also how to live with it daily. And it all starts with raising your awareness. Awareness is your path to personal power.

Bob Proctor
Master Success Coach;
Bestselling Author of
You Were Born Rich

INTRODUCTION

"An unexamined life is not worth living"
— Aristotle

THE DIFFERENCE BETWEEN AWARENESS AND SIMPLE-AWARENESS

Awareness is having a clear perception of your personality, including strengths, weaknesses, thoughts, beliefs, motivations, and emotions. ***Simple-Awareness*** is the ability to feel and to be *conscious* of events.

In developing both your awareness and simple-awareness you will become your most authentic self, which is the ultimate feeling of fulfillment. Before you dive into this book and begin building the groundwork for fulfillment, it is of the utmost importance that we explain what the differences are between awareness and simple-awareness. If you were to ask ten different people to define these terms, you would likely end up with ten different answers. For that reason, we will begin this book by explaining to you how we define these terms and how we have differentiated them. Awareness is the word used most often, but most people don't know that there are two types of awareness and that they differ immensely.

Awareness is an inner understanding of your thoughts, feelings, and emotions. The only way to become aware is to take the time to reflect on your thoughts, feelings, and emotions as an objective observer. Through awareness, you will also be able to dig deeper into the meaning behind why you act the way you do, and you will discover a new-found purpose in people, places, and things that you otherwise would have never experienced. Without reflection, we lose our ability to grow; and, if you stop growing, you stop becoming your authentic self. If you have not been aware for much of your life, becoming aware will likely bring you realizations about what your true purpose in life really is and who you are as your authentic self. In a study done by Tasha Eurich, while writing her book *Insight,* she discovered that ninety percent of people believe that they are aware, but after further investigation only ten percent of people actually turned out to be aware. This means that eighty percent of people are lying to themselves daily. If you have picked up this book, it is likely that you are not as aware as you may think. That is not meant to be taken negatively by you; by picking up this book in the first place, it means you realize the importance of awareness, which is a sign of being aware. Like any program you stick to, whether that be a diet, exercise, or educational program, if you are focused on seeing it through and staying disciplined, then you will become better as a result. The same goes for reading this book. Readers are among the most aware people on the planet, and so by reading a book written for helping you become more aware, we assure you it will happen. As you begin to develop your skills mentally, spiritually and physically, you may come to find that growth is the ultimate prize.

We all have weaknesses, just like we all have strengths, but only the most aware among us will be able to determine what makes us our best and our worst. Learning how to spot your deficiencies and strengths will give you the knowledge you need to develop the skills that make you your most authentic self. Without this knowledge, how will you know where to focus your time? How will you know what motivates you? How will you understand your thoughts, beliefs, and emotions? Through increased awareness you will learn to understand what is and is not in your control; simply put, awareness is understanding. Once you realize that you have no control over any external situation, but that you have absolute control over the way you act towards the situation, you will ultimately come to the realization that you are the author of your own life, and that it is your decisions that determine your destiny. You cannot rewrite the previous chapters of your life, but with an increase in awareness, you will be able to write the rest of your chapters any way you like.

Simple-awareness is quite different from awareness; it is the ability to understand your present experience as it is. As the famous author and British philosopher Alan Watts wrote, "You have to see and feel what you are experiencing as it *is*, and not as it is named." In other words, to be simply-aware, you must be fully present in your experience, and you must not *try* to feel, think, or listen because in doing so you are not actually feeling, thinking, or listening. As you are scrolling through your Instagram feed, you are not thinking about how you are looking at pictures, you are simply looking at them. However, if you were to think about yourself looking at the pictures, you would no longer be simply-aware of the picture presented in front of you. Instead, you would have become aware of your thoughts and feelings about the picture. You cannot separate yourself from an experience without moving on to another; you will either have to look at the picture or think about looking at the picture, you cannot do both at the same time.

This begs the question of whether we can be aware of past experiences or memories. To which we would have to respond, no. Try to remember a past experience, for example, of the last time you went to a restaurant. Now, let us ask you this, what are you aware of? You are no longer actually at the restaurant, and so you can no longer converse with your friends or family, ask for more water, or change your mind about your meal before the server gets to your table. This suggests that you are not actually looking at the past, for to look at the past would be impossible as it does not exist anymore. What you are actually doing is looking at a present trace of the past (a memory). From these types of memories, we like to think that we can relive an experience, which is not possible as one cannot re-experience an experience. We cannot be aware of the past because we can only experience it as part of the present. Understanding this should free your mind from thinking in the past, allowing you to be aware of this present moment.

> *"The capital-T Truth is about life BEFORE death. It is about the real value of a real education, which has almost nothing to do with knowledge, and everything to do with simple awareness; awareness of what is so real and essential, so hidden in plain sight all around us, all the time, that we have to keep reminding ourselves over and over:*
>
> *'This is water.'*
>
> *'This is water.'*
>
> *It is unimaginably hard to do this, to stay conscious and alive in the adult world day in and day out."*
>
> — *David Foster Wallace*

It would be hard to argue against Wallace's idea of the "capital-T Truth," especially when writing a book about awareness, and simple-awareness is the Truth. There is real value in staying conscious in adult life; and, as Wallace points out, it can be unimaginably hard to do so. Higher consciousness can be achieved by anyone; however, some people go through their entire lives without experiencing higher levels of consciousness, while for others it can happen suddenly or over a prolonged period of time. Many factors play a role, such as health choices, lifestyle, habits, ego, external events, and the people you are surrounded by. Different people become aware of higher consciousness at different times, usually based on a physical, emotional, or spiritual event that impacts them either positively or negatively. This is what we call an awakening! Once you awaken, there is no going back; it is now up to you to make the correct choices in lifestyle and habits to further develop into your most authentic self.

Many of us spend an entire lifetime without ever experiencing the awakening needed to begin to develop higher consciousness and increased awareness. Every single person is connected and intertwined with the divine source, or infinite intelligence, or the mind, or God (as defined by your own beliefs of what God may mean to you), and this is why it is possible for anyone to achieve higher levels of consciousness. But many people are brainwashed and kept "asleep," leaving them disconnected from their higher consciousness. The foods we eat, alcohol and drugs, overpowered egos, and, of course, media propaganda (the news, social media, TV shows, porn, etc.) are all factors that get in the way of people experiencing an awakening. In this book, we provide you with the tools and ideas that are necessary to help you turn off the noise and enter a state of mind and being in which the likeliness of experiencing an awakening will be far greater.

To be fulfilled, one must understand how to use awareness and simple-awareness to develop a higher consciousness. We believe that it is possible for each and every person to live a fulfilled life; we all have different passions and desires and so to say that not everyone can be fulfilled is to be ignorant to the fact that we are all different. We can all be fulfilled because we all feel fulfillment in different ways—it just takes learning how to use awareness and simple-awareness to our advantage.

In this book, you will begin to throw away your old definitions of what commonplace words like "happiness" and "success" mean to you, and you will redefine them in your own words. Your current definitions have likely been formed based on your environment and social conditioning over time, and so it is time to forget about how others say you should live your life and instead be true to yourself. After you redefine these words, you may come to the realization that you are much more likely to obtain happiness and success because now, instead of chasing someone else's ideas that you have been conditioned to desire, you will be chasing the goals and vision that your most authentic self has created.

Growth happens in the right places and for the right reasons the more we become aware. Whether your goal is to become better at your job, connect more effectively with people, become a champion, improve your health and fitness, increase your spirituality, or become your most authentic self, then awareness is the foundation.

Becoming simply-aware can ironically be complicated, yet once understood, it becomes very simple. It is to feel and understand yourself in the present moment, to simply see what you are looking at for what it *is* and not for what your thoughts about it are. If you are thinking about what has happened using present traces of the past, you are trying to become more aware. Anytime you are thinking about what is happening, happened, or may happen, you are not in a state of simple-awareness; instead, you are in a state of thinking—thinking that, when used correctly, will increase your awareness. It is common for people to misuse the word "awareness," and that is why we have separated this book into sections.

This book is a combination of ideas from successful men and women of the past, and includes many ideas that we have discovered through our own journeys of self-development. We have discovered many patterns in famous writings, which we have tied together to create this book with the hope of helping the world become aware, both simply and of the self. You will be doing a lot of reflection, so make sure to take your time and really think about what you are reading and how it makes you feel.

The content throughout this book will help you become aware of your strengths and weakness, not only in day-to-day activities but in the areas of your life (physical, mental, and spiritual) that are of the utmost importance to your happiness and health. We will help you develop your skill set, your ideas and beliefs, and your daily rituals and routines by giving you prescriptions at the bottom of certain subheadings. When you see the symbol "*Rx*," know that what follows is a prescription to help develop a skill, idea, or habit. These prescriptions are unlike the ones your doctor will give you; our prescriptions are meant to fix your problems not just mask them.

"Do you know that all the knowledge you'll ever need to do anything you want to do, you've already got? All you must do is develop your AWARENESS"

- Proctor Gallagher Institute

Awareness - The Poem

Awareness is about your personal story
Simple-Awareness is a totally different category
Awareness is about cultivating an undivided mind
Simple-Awareness is about everything and
nothing at the exact same time
Awareness will bring you closer to your authentic self
Simple-Awareness is simply the act of being thyself
Awareness requires objective observation
Simple-Awareness requires nothing but fixation
Fixation on the present moment, not the future or the past
Whereas, Awareness takes it all into account by way of contrast
An increased Awareness will surely lead to a brighter future
In which moments of Simple-Awareness become much smoother

AWARENESS - THE MOVEMENT

- Raise your simple-awareness so that you can enjoy life more NOW.
- Raise your awareness so that you can improve your life situation.
- Help you combine the two practices of awareness to live your life in a state of flowing fulfillment.

SECTION 1

MAKING SENSE OF THE "SELF"

THERE IS NO "SELF" WITHOUT THE "OTHER"

We have been conditioned to believe that our "self" is our thoughts and everything that lies beneath the surface of the skin. These are both parts of the "self" but they are small parts of the "self" in comparison to what the "self" really is. According to cognitive neuroscientists, the thoughts you consciously have throughout the day make up only five percent of cognitive activity. The other ninety-five percent of brain activity goes beyond conscious awareness. This should make you question why most of us form our self-identity through our conscious thoughts. To identify yourself simply from your conscious thoughts would be like predicting the end result of a math test with one hundred questions on it after only answering five of them. By identifying yourself with your thoughts, you are missing out on the deeper meaning of being a human.

The reason that most people will never transcend the standard definition of the "self" is because it can be scary to think about who and what you are without a self-identity that has been formed by past events and past thoughts. Even people who are not happy with their life situation as it is right now will likely be hesitant to give up their identity due to their fear of having no identity at all. The thought of having no identity can be scary, we understand that, but you must remember that you are *thinking* it would be

1

scary, which again only makes up five percent of cognitive brain activity. Stop letting your limited thinking control you, when you could transcend limited thinking and feel as though your "self" is a part of everything and everyone?

In its purest form, the "self" is everything. The book you hold in your hands is part of your "self," and the chair you sit on is a part of your "self;" you would not be who you are right now in this moment without the book you hold or the chair you sit in; therefore, you are them. This goes for other people as well—your friends and family members are all a part of your "self" just as much as you are part of their "self." Your friends and family have impressed upon the ninety-five percent of your brain activity that you are not consciously aware of; therefore, even though you are not aware of it, they are a part of your "self." Without them, you would not be you. You may have heard the quote "love your enemies." Most of us read this quote and take it in the literal sense, and we think "why would I ever love my enemies? They are my enemies for a reason." This quote is not meant to be taken literally, and you should not love your enemies in the sense of giving them hugs and kisses; you should love them because without them you are not yourself. If all of your enemies were to disappear tomorrow, so would a big part of your "self," because without your enemies, you would not have the same meaning and purpose in life, and you would not have an external force pushing you to take action; therefore, your enemies are just as much a part of your "self" as are your thoughts, your physical body, your friends and family, and everything else in this world, from the book in your hand to the clouds in the sky. Make it a priority in your life to detach and dissociate from the small definition of the "self" that you have been conditioned to have. You are much more than that old definition—you are a part of everything, and everything is a part of you.

Disidentification and detachment does not mean that you are nothing and own nothing; disidentification and detachment means that you are everything and nothing owns you.

"ME" OR "I"?

"I can only think seriously of trying to live up to an ideal, to improve myself, if I am split into two pieces. There must be a good 'I' who is going to improve the bad 'me' and the tussle between the two will very much stress the difference between them."

— *Alan Watts*

This is why self-improvement is challenging, regardless of who you are, and no matter what you want to improve, there has to be a "good" you who is going to improve the "bad" you. This leads us to believe there is more than one "self." Have you ever talked to yourself in third person? Who are you talking to? And who is doing the talking? Consider the sentence "I cannot live with myself." There must be an "I" who cannot live with "thyself." Now, most of us can agree there are two main components that make up the "self"—the mind and the body. Fewer people would be inclined to agree that there is a third component that makes up the "self," which would be the soul. So, if we were to say to ourselves, "I cannot live with myself," there are a few different things that we could mean:

1. My body (physical) cannot live with my mind (mental)
2. My mind (mental) cannot live with my body (physical)
3. My spirit cannot live with my mind (mental)
4. My spirit cannot live with my body (physical)

If any one of these areas is off balance, you will likely feel the internal tussle between the "self." You need to become aware of and be able to identify which area (body, mind, or spirit) is off balance so that you can work towards developing skills, ideas, and practices that help improve the area you are weak in.

EGO

"Ego is an unhealthy belief in our own importance."

— *Ryan Holiday*

To make sense of the "self," we have to make sense of the ego, because the ego makes up a large portion of the conscious self or thinking mind. When we as humans use our minds to consciously think thoughts, we are almost always listening to our ego talk back. Most people are unaware that their ego plays a lead role in almost every decision, and it is because of this we need to become aware of the many forms our ego can take and how to control the ego instead of passively letting it control us. Our ego most often acts as an emotional security mechanism—it keeps us from making a "fool" of ourselves, which actually means it keeps us from trying things we may fail at. Unfortunately, due to the fact that we live in a modern society that has put a negative perception on failure, our ego usually wins the battle that takes place in our mind. Can you think of a time you were in a meeting or with a group of friends and you felt like you should speak up about something but did not for fear of being wrong or being embarrassed? You must become aware that it was your ego protecting you from feeling uncomfortable that kept you quiet. There is a saying "life begins at the end of your comfort zone," and if you want to begin to really *live* life, you have to become aware of your ego at the times it tells you to play it safe so that you can use your will to push beyond the fear. The first few times you do this it will probably be very scary, but the first time you succeed in quieting your ego and you speak from a place of vulnerability and discomfort, you will feel so happy and proud that you did it, and this will become your new normal. This feeling of pride comes from speaking your mind despite your ego trying to talk you out of it. In doing this, you will have acted as your authentic self.

The ego is a perceived identity that is rooted in fear. The assumption is that the world is against you. The ego assumes you live in a world of scarcity, which means you must compete to live rather than create the good life. In the eyes of the ego, the world is comprised of winners and losers, rich and poor, successful and unsuccessful. The ego's focus is from the outside in. It needs to justify itself to you through logic, and it will engage you in a mental debate to prove that it is right. It must have external results to feel good. "I will be happy when I am in a relationship, have lots of money, success, and the house of my dreams and not until that has happened," it says. Regardless of who we are, we all have an ego, some larger than others, but we all have one and so it is important to understand how much we let our ego control our decisions and perceptions in life.

To understand our ego more deeply, we can take a look at our closest relationships. How do you treat the people you are supposed to care about the most? How do you perceive the success and failure of others? Do you assume you are better than other people? If you are the type of person who cannot be happy for someone else's success, it is simply due to your egoic mind trying to comfort you from emotional pain. Oftentimes when we see others succeed, we consciously or unconsciously think to ourselves that we should be more successful, and so seeing someone else succeed reminds us of our lack of success. This pattern of thinking leads us to make comparisons where comparisons are not necessary, and it destroys our ability to feel the joy in someone else's victory. Next time you see someone succeed, instead of comparing yourself to them or coming up with reasons why they succeeded, like they are just naturally talented, which in reality is simply an excuse for yourself, just look at the elation on their face and smile with them, feel their joy, and you will soon realize you can bask in the success of others just as much as you can for your own successes.

A common side effect of achievement, or a new found level of self-confidence, is an inflated ego. Our ego is our greatest internal enemy, and we have to keep a close eye on it. You cannot learn what you think you already know. Unfortunately, a lot of people get to a point in their lives where they decide that they know everything they want to know. Anyone who stops learning new things has adopted an identity of themselves as the master. If you desire growth and want to become the most authentic version of yourself, it is clear that it is better to identify yourself as a student of life rather than the master. As a student, you are always open to new ideas. You do not let your ego get in the way of creating and developing new ways of thinking that could enhance your experiences in life. On the other hand, if you identify as the master, you will never be willing to listen to new ideas. It is likely you will come off as rude because the only opinion you think should be heard is your own. As you begin to learn more and more, you will start to realize that there is so much information for you to learn and that the more you learn, the more there is to learn. Stop telling yourself you know everything, you do not, start learning new things and you will quickly realize that it takes a whole new level of humility to understand that the more you learn the less you know. This can be overwhelming at first, but we like to think of it in a different way. Instead of being overwhelmed by the information overload that is available in the palm of your hand, be grateful for it, because in understanding that you can learn more than you once imagined, you will never be bored again!

People with an unhealthy belief in themselves will begin to develop a superiority complex; this is extremely dangerous for anyone who wants to continue to improve any area of their life— this is the ego in its most futile stage. As the superiority complex develops, you will begin to turn away friends and family, whether you are doing it intentionally or not. When these connections start to break down, you begin to lose your grounding and will begin to think you are better than you really are. As we all know, overconfidence in this sense will not lead to better outcomes in anything you do, whether it is music, sports, relationships, writing, or any other type of work. This is why it is of the utmost importance that we catch ourselves and get our ego in check before we isolate ourselves and it is too late. Dig deep into your close relationships, and build strong connections; if you do not, you will surely find yourself feeling lonely at the top and soon find yourself crashing down with nobody to love or support you. Remember that it is not all about you, and ask yourself how you can better serve the people around you. Do not be surprised when you see incredible results and transformations in your own life as you start to practice living a life with a healthy balance of ego; this will just be the universe rewarding you for your selflessness and service.

> *"Every day for the rest of your life you will find yourself at one of three phases: aspiration, success, or failure. You will battle the ego in each of them. You will make mistakes in each of them. You must sweep the floor every minute of every day. And then sweep again."*
>
> — *Ryan Holiday*

Rx: In order to figure out whether any of your life goals are ego driven or authentic, ask yourself this question, "Am I in control of the goal or is the goal in control of me?"

* If you are in control of the goal, it is authentic.
* If the goal is in control of you, it is driven by ego.

For example, my goal to own my dream home/sanctuary with all of my desires is a goal that is in control of me; it is ego driven.

Whereas my goal to write a book and produce a rap album is a goal that I am in control of; it is authentic.

Now it is important to understand that just because your goal is ego driven does not make it a bad goal; however, without authentic goals that support and build the foundation for your ego-driven goal to come true, it never will.

THE THREE LEVELS OF CONSCIOUSNESS

There are three levels of consciousness: Higher Consciousness, Ordinary Unconsciousness, and Deep Unconsciousness. Now we know assumptions are often ill advised, but in this case we are going to make one to help you understand the three different levels of consciousness. We are going to assume that five percent of people are highly conscious, ninety percent are ordinarily unconscious, and the remaining five percent are deeply unconscious. Imagine highly conscious people as those who take great care of their physical and mental health and who give back more than they take from society and the people around them. These people are happy and successful by their own definition. Ordinary Unconscious people make up the masses, or the majority. These people do not love their job, they look forward to time off from work, and they spend most of their downtime being unproductive/entertained. The easiest way to identify an ordinary unconscious person is if you hear them complaining, it is oftentimes about being bored; this is simply because they have no passion and purpose in their life. Deeply unconscious people are society's greatest problem. These people were once ordinarily unconscious, but due to a negative mental or physical emotional impact, such as a death in the family or the loss of a job, they have been pushed into a state of anger, rage, or depression. Someone who is deeply unconscious does not care about the well-being of others; they are a major risk to society in terms of causing others mental or physical pain.

Most ordinary unconscious people do not recognize that they are in this state of mind; however, subconsciously, they attempt to escape the unease of this state through drinking, drugs, food, sex, shopping, basically anything that will disrupt the mundaneness of their everyday life. You may be wondering what makes someone live like this. As far as we can tell, it all begins with conditioning since birth. That is not to say you cannot escape an ordinary unconscious state of mind; on the contrary, anyone can escape this state and become highly conscious, but the first step is becoming aware and recognizing that your mind is the most powerful tool you will ever have, and so there is a better way to live than to be bored or to complain. People in this state of ordinary unconsciousness have never taken the time to become aware, and, therefore, they never discover their true passion or purpose in life. These people are usually the ones who make excuses such as, "He or she was born that way," or "I am not smart enough or strong enough to do that," or "Some people have it and some people do not;" these are all just excuses that keep you asleep and prevent you from becoming highly conscious and aware. Becoming highly conscious and aware is a shocking and truth-revealing process. It means facing emotionally challenging pains from your past so that you can get to the root of your problems.

BE THE OBJECTIVE OBSERVER

The first step in personal liberation is to ask yourself, "Who is the witness of my conscious and ever-changing experience?" Objective observation is the understanding that you are the one who knows the knowing, rather than the one who knows the experience. In other words, you will become an objective observer as opposed to the reactive self. A growing problem in society is unconscious reactions to external situations. Why do you react and form sudden judgements about a situation that is not in your control and that will only contribute to the flow of negative thinking? Because you have not been consciously aware of the power of your mind... until now.

Have you ever listened in on your inner dialogue? Have you heard yourself thinking and been able to monitor your reactions to your thoughts and then dictate which thoughts came next? This is what is called being the objective observer. You have to become aware that you are in control of your thoughts and, therefore, how you respond to any and all situations. Your physical body could be thrown in prison; however, you will always be in complete control over your mind.

> *"Your true self is large and powerful and beautiful. Your body is your vehicle but it is not who you are. Your thoughts give you the ability to create your life but they are not who you are. If you can observe your thoughts and your body, then you are the observer. Who is the observer?"*
>
> — *Tamika Hilder*

Becoming aware of this will hopefully be as life changing for you as it was for us. Once we realized that we are all connected to something much greater than our thinking mind and physical body, we were able to control both our minds and bodies in a much more powerful way; we became highly conscious; we became the observers, and, consequently, we no longer reacted to external events but instead responded mindfully, whether that meant keeping our opinions to ourselves or expressing them authentically and constructively.

We have all had experiences where we let our anger or frustration get the better of us, and as a result said or did something that we later regret. This is because we let our reactive selves take control of our actions based on our emotions or feelings, which leads to actions that are not well thought through or mindful. As the objective observer, we are able to see the big picture; we can still feel our emotions, but we will be rational and take a moment to think things through using the *System 2* part of our brain before we make a decision on how to act. *System 2* is the effortful, slow, and controlled part of the brain that we use for problem solving and deep thinking. When *System 2* gets tired, it allows the part of our brain which is automatic, fast, and unconscious in its thinking to take over. This part of our brain is called *System 1* and is sometimes thought of as our lizard brain, which is responsible for the fight or flight response. The more fatigued we become, the less likely we are to observe our thoughts or a situation objectively, and as we become more fatigued, we let our lizard brain guide us towards subjective reactions.

Objective observation requires a heightened sense of awareness. Objective observation is how it sounds—it is the ability to observe our own thoughts and emotions in an objective manner, as opposed to how we normally observe ourselves, which is subjective. Objectivity is unbiased, so to be able to objectively observe your own thoughts and emotions will allow you to make clearer decisions based on what you value most. What you value is not always what you want in the moment. For example, if you are staring at a chocolate cake, it is likely you will want to eat some of it; however, if you value being healthy, you probably should not eat it. There are two simple ways to become the objective observer in this chocolate cake situation. First, you can ask yourself, "What would the best version of myself do right now?" Would he give in to temptation and eat the cake? Or would he stay disciplined to, and in alignment with, what he values?

If asking what the best version of yourself would do does not sound like it is something that would work for you, then you can simply imagine an indifferent spectator looking over your shoulder, always ready to provide you with advice that aligns with your values. You can imagine any person, dead or alive. You can even imagine a fictional character. It doesn't matter who or what you imagine as the indifferent spectator as long as you remember that they are always with you and always going to tell you to do what is best for you in the bigger picture. You may notice that the indifferent spectator is a similar concept to simply asking: what would the best version of myself do? And you would be right, because the concepts are similar. It is just that some people find it easier to imagine someone else supporting them and giving them advice as opposed to their own self. Regardless of which concept you like more, we sincerely hope that you will give this a try in your daily life, because having the ability to step outside of your normal subjective thoughts and desires is one of the greatest tools you can have for making decisions that align with your values.

Higher consciousness is not the thoughts in your mind that flow throughout the day, but the ability to acknowledge you are having those thoughts and observing them is highly conscious. Becoming aware that you are able to listen to your own thoughts creates a mental space to observe your thoughts before responding, thus constructing a mindful response.

Rx: Perceive life from the third person inside!

CONTROL YOURSELF

Awareness is a power; a power that allows you to see yourself for who you truly are and who you truly can be—the potential is nearly limitless. The more aware you become, the easier it will be for you to recognize the moments you are having a negative reaction to someone or something and be able to rapidly identify what is causing your reaction and why. For example, you get cut off in traffic; before you begin to lose your temper ask yourself, "Am I in control of this situation?" Of course you're not, so there is no reason to let the external event frustrate you; reacting to the situation will only make you feel worse and put you in a negative vibration.

The reason for this simple example is because it has happened to all of us. No one drives around wanting someone to cut them off, but when it does happen, you have to realize that although you have no control over the situation, you have full control over how you respond to it. Never let something outside of your control frustrate you. In doing so, you miss out on what it means to live. In a moment that you would normally be frustrated, like waiting in line at the grocery store, instead of complaining or getting frustrated by how long you will have to wait, ask yourself "What am I in control of, and what am I not in control of?" You will realize you are not in control of a lot of things, like how fast the line moves, or how many people are in line, but you will realize you are in control of your reaction to the situation and how you choose to respond to it. Someone who is highly conscious will use this time in line to connect with their breathing and become simply-aware of the moment, which will allow them to enjoy moments that were once thought of as annoying or a waste of time. Remember any time you are feeling frustrated to ask yourself, "What am I in control of, and what am I not in control of?" React and the situation will control you; respond and you are in control of the situation.

Rx: In any and all situations ask yourself, "What am I in control of and what am I not in control of?"

SECTION 2

IT'S TIME TO REFLECT

SELF-EXAMINATION

"We can't reimpose old myths on ourselves or believe in new ones made up out of a desire for comfort; therefore, the path of self-examination is the only one a person of conscience can reasonably follow."

— *Deepak Chopra*

This should bring comfort to all of us, as Deepak Chopra points out, "the path of self-examination is the only one a person of conscience can reasonably follow"; with that being said, self-examination is clearly an obvious path that one should follow if they wish to find fulfillment. Fortunately for those of you reading this book, the foundation for self-examination is awareness. When examining yourself, the only way to really understand who you are is to ask better questions—better questions that will give you better answers, which will make you more aware. These questions can be tough to answer because they may bring up past emotions that you have been trying to suppress for some time, but if you want to become truly fulfilled then you have no choice but to face yourself and ask the tough questions. Throughout this book, we will be providing you with some examples of questions that you can use for self-examination and to better understand who you are and what makes you feel fulfilled.

WHAT DOES FULFILLMENT FEEL LIKE?

Although the journey to fulfillment will be different for everyone, the feeling of fulfillment is similar for each of us. Fulfillment is a feeling of inner contentment, inner peace, and not wanting anything that is not currently within. Do not get fulfillment mixed up with satisfaction. Satisfaction will make you lazy, whereas fulfillment will be the rewarding feeling you get for taking actions that align with your values and purpose. A lifetime of fulfillment is attainable for anyone; all you have to do is work towards your purpose and let your values guide you.

You will need to become aware in order to be able to define your authentic values and true purpose. Without heightened levels of awareness, you will live in an ordinary unconscious state of mind. In this unconscious state, fulfillment is non-existent; it is replaced by feelings of pleasure in the form of instant gratification. You see many people give in to external temptations each day just so that they can feel a sense of pleasure. The problem with this way of living is that pain is inherent in pleasure; you cannot have one without the other. Whether it is the pleasure of drinking, drugs, unhealthy foods, a Netflix binge, or surface-level relationships, the pain will always be lurking in the shadows; it will form as a hangover, excess weight gain, shame, or emotional heartache.

Unfortunately, many people are stuck in an unhealthy unconscious loop, in which they are identified by their egoic mind. To escape this loop, you must be willing to disidentify from your past, and you must be willing to admit everything you are today is a result of your own decisions. This also means you have all of the power to become what you want and have what you want; you just need to accept that you are in charge of how you think and act. Your decisions, not your conditions, determine your destiny.

If you are someone who is tired of accepting the pain that follows pleasure and would like to feel fulfillment on a deep level, you must disidentify from your past and your egoic mind; instead, you must begin to identify yourself as the objective observer! We all have the awareness to listen to our thoughts, so spend some time listening in on your internal conversations. Discover what thoughts benefit you and what thoughts are no longer needed on your journey to inner peace and fulfillment.

LIVING FROM THE INSIDE OUT

> *"If an egg is broken by an outside force, life ends. If broken by an inside force, life begins. Great things always begin from the inside."*
>
> — *Jim Kwik*

The majority of people have been conditioned to live from the outside in, rather than the inside out. When we let our present results dictate our thoughts, which get impressed on our subconscious mind, our body is kept in the same vibration and that is why our results do not change. Instead of living through our intellectual faculties, imagination, perception, will, reason, intuition, and memory, we have been conditioned to live through our sensory factors: sight, sound, smell, taste and touch. While these sensory factors are important, they do not allow us to come close to using our full potential. We need to learn to use our intellectual factors if we want to live up to our potential. We want you to become aware that we all have these intellectual faculties, or mental muscles, which are like any other muscle—they need to be developed or they will become weak. The next six subsections cover each of our six intellectual faculties and give you a prescription for strengthening them.

IMAGINATION

"Imagination is the most marvelous, miraculous, inconceivably powerful force that the world has ever known."

— *Napoleon Hill.*

Most of us are aware of our imagination—it is where we dare to dream and fantasize. When we were young, we would use our imagination all the time while playing, and we could turn any old object like a stick or a rock into whatever we wanted. Unfortunately, as we got older, we were told to stop dreaming and pay attention to what is "real." From that point on, the imagination began to fade, and before you knew it, you stopped using your imagination altogether.

We need to take our minds back to a time when we used to use imagination. As adults, we begin to ignore the most powerful force the world has ever known: the imagination. This is detrimental to our long-term success and fulfillment. We as human beings need to use our imaginations to visualize where we want to be and what we want to do. If you are the type of person who is lacking imagination, do not be surprised if your vision is unclear when you close your eyes. This is just because you have shut off the creative and imaginative part of your mind for so long that you are going to have to put in some time to get it back. It is not hard work, it just requires time—time spent with your eyes closed in a quiet room, just you and your mind.

Rx: Go into a dark quiet room and visualize everything you want in life, and bring clarity and feeling to your vision, as if you already had it.

PERCEPTION

Perception is our belief from our own point of view. People like to get in arguments all the time trying to prove who is right and who is wrong, but a lot of the time a simple change in perspective is all that is needed. Imagine a piece of paper with writing on one side. Now if you were holding this piece of paper with writing on one side and held it up to someone with the blank side facing them and asked "Is there anything written on this piece of paper, yes or no?" They would say "no" and think you were dumb, but if you turned the sheet of paper over and showed them the blank side, they would suddenly perceive the same thing you were. No one was right or wrong in this scenario, which should make you think about the fact that there is not always a right or wrong answer. The next time you get into an argument about something, just stop and try to see it from the other person's perspective.

Rx: If you have a problem or challenge, write it on a piece of paper and put the paper in the middle of a table. Look at it and ask yourself, "Is this problem in me or on the paper?" Then look at it from someone else's point of view. "How would my father look at this? How would David look at this? How would Myles look at this?" From there, see what you can come up with.

WILL

The will gives us the ability to concentrate. With all the distractions we get in this day and age, it is easy to get off track and lose focus on the task at hand. When we develop the will, we are able to get done what needs to get done. Many of us think we can multitask, but this is simply not true—you can only focus on one thing at a time. When we try to multitask, nothing really gets completed. We just have a bunch of things on the go. In the modern world of smartphones, where our focus is constantly being pulled in different directions, being able to focus on one thing at a time has become more important than ever. It is what we like to call "butt power," which is having the ability to stay in one spot and concentrate until a job is done. This is a skill that very few of us have anymore, and it continues to diminish as technology has become a pillar of society. To be able to thrive in today's world, you need to be able to silence the noise and use your willpower to focus on the task at hand.

Rx: Place a candle opposite your favourite chair. Put a timer on for five minutes and stare at the flame. Keep staring at the flame for the entire five minutes. You will notice that your mind will wander. Do not get upset; just bring your focus back to the flame. At first you might only be able to focus for a couple seconds at a time before your mind starts to wander, but as you keep doing this day after day for ninety days, you will develop a very strong will. The key here is to do it for ninety days straight. If you skip a day, then you have to start back at day one.

REASON

The reasoning mind is our thinking, or conscious, or intellectual, mind. We have an enormous amount of thoughts coming into our mind all the time, and it is with your reasoning faculty that you can accept or reject the thoughts that come to your mind. The majority of us do not use our reasoning faculties to accept or reject thoughts; instead, we allow whatever the outside world is telling us to filter right into the subconscious mind, and then we get emotionally involved with things we probably wouldn't have if we had used reason; this is the definition of living from the outside in. The next time someone is telling you something that is not serving you, just say to yourself, "I reject this information," and on the outside you can say to the person "interesting," and then let go of the information. You could also change the subject and talk about something that the person is good at, which will provide a smooth transition between talking points.

Rx: Purposefully place yourself in situations where you will need to use your reasoning mind to consciously and mindfully interact with other people or deal with the situation.

INTUITION

Intuition is the direct perception of truth, and it does not allow for fear. The assumption is that you are perfectly safe and secure as you are. Intuition knows that you live in a world of abundance, and to get whatever it is you want and need, you need not look for happiness outside of yourself. It assumes there is plenty to go around, and that when you gain, so does everyone else. Intuition comes from the inside. It urges you toward joyful self-expression. Intuition is heart-centered. It does not bother with justification, because it expects you to recognize it as truth. If you try to argue with it, it will give you the same answer again and again.

Here are a couple of examples of the differences between your intuitive mind and your egoic mind...

- Intuition will guide you into starting a business or project that helps people. Ego will guide you towards ventures based on fame and fortune.
- Intuition will guide you to lose weight and increase muscle mass to become healthier. Ego will guide you to lose weight so that you look good at the beach.
- Intuition will guide you to ask someone you find attractive and kind on a date. Ego will guide you to do this for pleasure, and so that you will not be alone.

The voice you hear may sound similar, but you will attract totally different outcomes depending on the intent behind your actions.

When you listen to the voice of your ego, you will be fueled by feelings of fear or power. When you listen to the voice of intuition, you will invite the flow of love, self-peace, and abundance into your life. Your intuition enables you to tune into the energy of the universe by sensing vibrations. You can also use it to "read" other people, since everyone is a mass of vibrating energy.

You are probably wondering, "How do I know where my intuition comes from and how do I develop it?" Start paying attention to the things you normally would not. Notice the feelings and thoughts you have in situations that you would normally dismiss. These feelings, hunches, and coincidences are all messages from the universal mind (the creator), meant to guide you in the direction towards your most authentic self. Listen to these messages as the conscious observer, and you will be shocked at the number of times your thoughts lead you astray, especially if the thoughts are coming from your egoic mind. Make sure you take the time to reflect on your thoughts and feelings so that you get a better understanding of where your thoughts and feelings are coming from. If you feel anxious or tense based on your thoughts in a situation, it is likely your egoic mind guiding you, whereas if you are uplifted and loving, then it is likely your intuition guiding you.

> *"The intuitive mind is a sacred gift and the rational mind is a faithful servant.*
>
> *We have created a society that honors the servant and has forgotten the gift."*
>
> — *Albert Einstein*

Rx: When you are talking to someone, give them all your conscious attention. Don't think about your next question or if your shirt makes you look fat. Give them your undivided attention, and you will be able to pick up their energy.

MEMORY

You will find that most people say they have a terrible memory, but that is not true. We all have a great memory; we just need to develop it. If you want to remember a speech, or lyrics to a song, you can remember them. It will simply take repetition and the will to focus.

Our experience in life may depend on the memories we carry throughout our life, especially if you are someone who spends most of their time living in the past. This unnecessary baggage that some of us carry as memories is weighing us down. If you are not remembering it to learn from it, then forget it.

Rx: Repetition is the first law of learning, so if you want to remember, repeat it.

Rx: Take a look back at your memories. If they do not serve you, let them go because they are doing you no good.

STRENGTHS & WEAKNESSES

One thing that all people who show signs of being highly aware have in common is their ability to self-diagnose not only their strengths but also their weaknesses. Most people will be able to tell you what they think their strengths are, but if you were to ask about their weaknesses, you may be surprised to hear that most people do not know what their weaknesses are. They will probably be able to tell you what they do not like about themselves, usually in a joking or sarcastic manner, but they do not know the weaknesses that have caused them to be the way they are. Weaknesses are hard to determine. They are not obvious to us like our strengths, but that is simply because we do not perceive our weaknesses to be as sexy as our strengths, and so even though our weaknesses are oftentimes in plain sight, they are not so obvious to ourselves because we would rather focus on anything but that which makes us weak. If you take some time to make yourself aware of your weaknesses, and then work hard to become competent in those areas, you will be doing something that most people will never do.

If you are struggling to uncover your weaknesses, do not hesitate to ask a friend or family member for feedback. All you have to do is ask them, "What do you think are three of my strengths and three of my weaknesses?" Yes, ask about the strengths too, as others can see what is hidden in our blind spots. Getting objective and constructive feedback from a trusted friend or family member will make your job of becoming aware of your strengths and weaknesses a little bit easier. It is not over after that, though. It is just getting started. You need to constantly be aware of what your strengths and weaknesses are as they change throughout the course of your life. As you become competent in areas you were once weak, you will discover that other areas of weakness appear and can be worked on.

Now, when we are talking about our weaknesses, we want you to think of ones that will help you get to where you want to go. If you are weak in writing and you want to become a professional football player then that probably is not a weakness you need to improve upon. As for your strengths, they are your strengths for a reason, so triple down on them, and do whatever it is you are strong in as much as you can. Not only because this is likely going to be where you will see the most success but also because it is most likely an area of your life that you enjoy quite a lot.

Rx: List three strengths and three weaknesses below.

STRENGTHS:

_____

_____

_____

WEAKNESSES:

_____

_____

_____

THE KNOWING DOING GAP

Every single one of us can relate to the Knowing Doing Gap. This is when you do something you know you should not be doing and yet still do it anyways, or, knowing you *should* be doing something and not doing it. A good example of this would be trying to live a healthy lifestyle in terms of nutrition. Imagine a whole pizza and a couple pieces wouldn't hurt you, but you end up eating the whole pizza. You know you probably should not eat it, yet you do it anyways and feel guilty about it afterwards. If you were to ask yourself why you ate it, your answer would most likely be "I don't know."

Why do we do these things to ourselves, especially when we know better? Well, it is our paradigm, our habits, it is that little voice inside our head saying, "Go ahead and eat the pizza, it will not hurt me," or "I have worked hard enough, I should reward myself." When that little voice is talking, you need to remember what your purpose is (you will discover this in Section 3, under the subsection, Develop Your Passion & Turn it into your Purpose), and then use self-discipline in the form of willpower until you have changed your habit. To tighten up the gap between knowing and doing, you will need to change your paradigm, and you will literally need to make the action of doing become a habit. How to change your paradigm is covered in the next section, Section 3: Becoming Aware.

As we get older, we tend to know more and do less, which is the cause of most stress and unease among people. With that being said, it is your job in life to convert what you know into what you do. The most successful people in the world aren't always the smartest, but they are always the person who does what needs to be done. Do not get caught up in the idea that you need to know everything before you get started. You could know everything there is to know about exercise, but if you do not get started, then you may as well know nothing. Too many people let their knowledge outweigh their actions. Do not be one of those people; instead, find a balance between what you know and what you do.

YOUR NARRATIVE MATTERS

Those who lack awareness will tell themselves stories about why someone else has a better life than them, and the story tends to relate to a lack of opportunities due to a lack of money or resources, or because they have bad genetics. These same people blame others for their lack of happiness and success and tend to make excuses as a coping mechanism because they do not take pride in their life the way it is right now. Blaming others for the reason why you are not who or where you want to be in life is one of the most toxic ways of thinking any human can have. These types of thoughts will tear you away from focusing on what truly matters and will block you from living the life you could have.

> *"People are always blaming their circumstances for what they are. I don't believe in circumstances. The people who get on in this world are the people who get up and look for the circumstances they want, and if they can't find them, they make them."*
>
> — *George Bernard Shaw*

Looking back, we have both realized we grew up blaming our circumstances on our family and school systems, which was not doing us any favours. In reality, there was no one else to blame but ourselves. Our family did the best they could with what they had and what they knew, and the same goes for the school system. If you blame others for the reason you are where you are and who you are today, we are writing this to tell you that it is that very narrative which will do you no good if you have any desire to grow and thrive in your life. Our decisions and our actions determine who and what we become, not our conditions or our environment. The moment we blame conditions for who we are, we have begun losing the battle that will forever take place in our mind. Our narrative about who we are is more important than anything else in this world; our narrative controls our decisions and actions. So, if you are the type of person who is currently engaged in self-sabotage in the form of self-talk that leads you to believe circumstances have dictated who you are, then this is your wake-up call to change your mindset and realize that you are in control of your decisions, actions, and reactions, and, therefore, you are in control of who you are and who you become.

"We are all self-made, but only the successful will admit it"

— *Earl Nightingale*

VALUES

If we were to ask you what your values are, would you be able to give us an answer? We live in a world that is so focused on goals, we often completely forget about values. Values are a person's principles, or standards of behaviour. Values are an authentic judgment of what one finds important in life.

People often set a goal to become rich and famous so that they can afford what they want and do what they want, where they want, but that does not mean they will act in a way that is in accordance with their values to achieve that goal, especially if they have never taken the time to determine a set of values. Sometimes people will achieve their goal only to find themselves feeling empty, or guilty and shameful about the way they achieved it, and this is likely because the goal never aligned with their authentic values, had they set any. Some people confuse goals and values; the easiest way to differentiate them is by understanding that goals are finite, and that they have an ending. Whereas values dictate the principles of life that you live by; values are infinite, but this does not mean that they do not change over the course of your life. Values are something that will always be a part of you and will guide you along your journey.

Having goals is an important part of life, and it is great that most of us have them, but it is unfortunate that most people do not know what their values are. It is as simple as taking some time to think about how you want to live your life, which is different from your usual thoughts about what you want out of life. If you take a few minutes at the end of this section to create your own set of values and then keep them in the forefront of your mind when being and doing things, you will increase your chances of living your life how you want while also getting what you want, thus becoming fulfilled. When you are taking action that aligns with your values, you will feel motivated and pulled towards your goals; as opposed to the feeling most people have, which is constantly pushing towards their goals, which produces little progress. When you act in accordance with your values, your actions will become more powerful and you will become more authentic. Simply put, when you act with your values in mind, you are acting as the best version of yourself.

MY VALUE SYSTEM

- _____
- _____
- _____

- _____
- _____
- _____
- _____
- _____
- _____
- _____

Rx: Think about how you want to live your life, not what you want out of it.

WANT TO VS. HAVE TO

When we set any type of goal, whether it be to lose thirty pounds, run a marathon, meditate every day, or stop judging people, we will be much more likely to achieve the goal if it is something we want to do, as opposed to something we have to do. This is because it is very likely we will have to change some habits to reach our goal. Think about a time you told yourself you had to do something. You likely had to use willpower to take certain actions and use even more willpower not to take certain actions. The reason you had to use willpower is because the goal you set to accomplish was likely formed due to social conditioning—it is something you wanted to achieve so that others would think of you differently. These types of goals, while they may be what you should do to become a better version of yourself, are not authentic unless they align with your values. So, you may decide to lose thirty pounds because your spouse or friends think it's the right thing to do, but unless you have a personal reason that aligns with your values, then you will constantly be pushing towards your goals instead of being pulled towards them. If you have children, and you value being around to support them both physically and mentally for as long as you can, then the goal of losing weight will be something you will value as long as you believe that being overweight is unhealthy and could become a barrier for quality time spent with your children. Remember you will have to commit to changing your habits if you want to achieve the goal. When you no longer have to lose weight, but instead you want to, the goal of losing weight will no longer need a numerical value such as thirty pounds; your goal will simply be to make health a habit, and soon a lifestyle, simply because what you truly value is spending more quality time with your family. We all have the same twenty-four hours in a day, but what sets us apart from one another are our daily habits. You may think you do not have time to be physically active or to work on developing yourself either mentally or spiritually because you have a nine-to-five obligation, but the truth is most people have a job and yet many of them still find the time to improve themselves; anyone can replace any bad habit with a good habit if they really want to.

Rx: Ask yourself, "Do I really want this? Or am I telling myself I have to do this?" If you really want something, you will change your habits to achieve it. Do not take action just because you feel like you have to or that you should; take action because you want to, and that way you will enjoy it and you can make it a habit.

WHAT MOTIVATES YOU?

There are five levels of motivation, and your actions and feelings will greatly depend on which level you are on. It is important to understand the five levels of motivation so that you can determine the level you are currently on and then work towards the fifth level. The five levels of motivation, in order from the least powerful to the most powerful are: Fear, Power, Results, Duty/Responsibility, Love.

We are all at different levels of motivation, but what we are bringing your awareness towards is that love is, and always will be, the most powerful motivator. Unfortunately, much of society these days is built by people who are motivated by power and results, and the people that work for them are motivated by fear. People can feel multiple levels of motivation at the same time, and you can also feel different levels of motivation depending on what situation you are in. What we mean by this is just because you are motivated by fear or power in one area, does not mean you cannot be motivated by duty or love in another.

Rx: Ask yourself what you are motivated by at work? At home? At the gym? While playing games or sports? Just make sure you ask yourself what level of motivation you are on, because in doing this you will be one step closer to answering why you do what you do.

SECTION 3

BECOMING AWARE

WRITE IT DOWN

Everyone wants to be fulfilled, YES, everyone wants to be loved, YES, everyone wants to be healthy, YES, everyone wants to be wealthy, YES, everyone wants to be successful, YES, and everyone wants to feel meaning in their life, YES! These are all things we can universally agree on. Where many of us will begin to disagree is where the power comes from to live a life of fulfillment, love, health, success and meaning as well as what makes someone feel any of these things. From person to person, fulfillment and success can look and feel very different. It seems that, over time, many definitions have developed for these words, which is a good thing. This just means there is more than one way to be fulfilled or feel successful. It is important that you take a moment to write down and redefine success and fulfillment when we ask you to, because through redefining these terms for yourself, you will be taking steps towards becoming highly conscious and self-aware.

Most people think that there is something external that brings success and happiness into the lives of a select group of lucky people. These people would be wrong. Success and happiness are felt internally and can only be created through inner strength. As the Navy Seal David Goggins says, *"Inner strength is not found, it's created."* External things cannot fix internal issues such as happiness, love, prosperity, success, and meaning. If you find yourself struggling in any of these areas, stop wasting your time trying to cover up the issue with something external, it will only do just that, cover it up. Everything is temporary, and when that cover comes off, you will still have to fix the internal issue before you can level up your happiness, love, health, success, and meaning in a lasting, fulfilling way. The first step in fixing the internal issue is to write; by redefining and writing down in your own words some of the terms we have mentioned throughout this chapter you will begin to grow internally.

Neither of us was ever one to put pen to paper. Teachers would always say "write it down, because you will forget." And sure enough, we would forget if we did not write it down. Maybe it was because we had no interest in what we were being told to write down, and that is a totally different story, but what we have come to realize is...

Writing causes thinking
Thinking creates an image
Images control feelings
Feelings cause actions
Actions create RESULTS

Until you redefine the terms listed on the next page, you will always be the consumer. The consumer is unaware of the path he or she is on; they might think they are working towards being fulfilled and successful, but if they have not defined what fulfillment and success is for them, they will be working towards someone else's definition of fulfillment and success. Those who make it to the final destination of what someone else has defined as success or fulfillment will find themselves feeling empty and without meaning, despite reaching what they thought were their goals. In hindsight, they were someone else's goals, whether that is society, the media, or friends and family. If you are trying to live a fulfilled life, you cannot be following a path towards a vision that was not created by yourself.

The motivational speaker Zig Ziglar once said, *"You can't hit a target you cannot see, and you cannot see a target you do not have."* So, if you go through your entire life without having defined for yourself what your target for fulfillment or success is, then we promise you, you will never hit it. However, now that you have become aware, you can find peace in knowing that you are one step closer to living the life you want and becoming your most authentic self.

There is no denying that human beings are creatures of habit, and the habits we have control much of the way we live, and so it is extremely important to have habits that attract you to the life you want. Whether you desire happiness, success, love, or money, it all comes down to your habits. In a world where the media has done a really great job of portraying an image of success and happiness to a global audience, it is important to take a step back and detach yourself from what others think; instead, live by your own definitions. It all starts when you redefine your life by writing it down...

Internal Success:

_____

_____

_____

External Success:

_____

_____

_____

Failure:

_____

_____

_____

Fulfillment:

_____

_____

_____

Rx: Get yourself a journal or use the notes app on your smart-device to write down your thoughts and feelings; just do it!

PARADIGMS RUN YOUR LIFE

A paradigm is a multitude of habits stored in a section of our subconscious mind. We are all being controlled by our paradigms, a mental program that has almost exclusive control over our habitual behaviour, and almost all our behaviour is habitual. Our paradigms are programmed right from birth through genetic and environmental conditioning. Although our genetics predispose us to certain illnesses and conditions, there is a big difference between being predisposed and predetermined. Our environment plays a much bigger role in who we become than was once thought. The genetic conditioning is why we look so much like our relatives, but when we make our debut, our subconscious mind is wide open, taking in all the information around us through relationships with adults, peers, teachers, and the media. If you took a baby from Vancouver, Canada, and let it grow up in Madrid, Spain, that baby would have no recognition of the English language and vice versa.

We change our paradigms through repetition, or an emotional impact. An emotional impact can be something positive, but it is usually something negative, like a death in the family or loss of a job. We have been programmed since birth with other people's habits, including our parents, friends, the media, and many others. These habits control the way we think and act without us even realizing it. Think of when you put your pants on in the morning. You do not even realize it, but if you are not thinking, you will put the same foot in first every time. This is because before you could dress yourself, your parents would dress you and they would put your pants on the same way they would put their own pants on. Try putting your other foot in first, it feels awkward. Be careful you might lose your balance. We chose this as an example because life doesn't get much simpler than putting your pants on. However, it would still take a conscious effort to put them on starting with your opposite foot. This is just one of the many examples of the ways we are conditioned. We are all capable of changing the habits/ paradigms that we have been conditioned to have. It will simply come down to two things: first being able, and next being willing. We are all able, but are you willing?

> *"To be able to shape your future, you have to be WILLING and ABLE to change your paradigm."*
>
> — *Joel Barker*

Paradigms - The Poem

The ones we currently have are old and outdated
The time for change is now, that can't be debated
We can all do better, that's a phrase I believe in
So stop blaming others, instead give your mindset a spin
Forming new patterns is the way to begin
Repetition is the surest way to change your paradigm
Make the conscious effort and you will see results in no time

REPROGRAM YOUR MIND

The most common way the mind is reprogrammed is simply through repetition, so if you want to change a paradigm, replace your negative action with a positive action and do it over and over and over again until it becomes a habit. You may have heard that it only takes two weeks to form a habit, but the timing may differ from person to person. Two weeks usually works well as a general guideline for creating and getting rid of any habits. Let's use social media as an example. Social media is a great tool; you can get your message out to a lot of people in so many ways, and it is a lot faster than the old fashion way of spreading a message through word of mouth. But this tool can also become an addiction—an addiction that makes us ignorant to the real world. A lot of people are on all sorts of social media platforms all day, every day, and this is becoming problematic because it is destroying people's ability to focus and be productive by keeping them otherwise preoccupied. People are getting emotionally involved with a lot of useless, negative, unrealistic information and images that are programming their minds in a negative way. When we read or watch a video clip about something negative, we let that negativity flow right into our subconscious mind. That puts us in a negative vibration, and, from there, we will attract negative things into our lives. Most of us are probably unaware of how social media could have reprogrammed our minds without us even making a conscious choice, but it has without a doubt reprogrammed the minds of many.

The older generation will claim that they are better off because they do not use social media, but that same person watches the news at the same time every day and that can produce an even worse result than social media. On social media you get to choose what type of content you see and hear, whereas on the news, the negativity is forced down your throat whether you like it or not; the only relief from the negativity is the weather forecast, but if it happens to be raining, then that will often affect people in a negative way as well. You picked up this book for a reason. If you are someone who is still a common viewer of the news, we suggest you turn it off for good, replace it with educational podcasts or motivational videos, and if you do not decide to replace the news, just remember it is your choice on how you program your mind and what you program it with, then ask yourself, "Am I programming my mind to be its best?"

We all have choices each day regarding what we listen to, what we watch, and what we read, and all this information plays a key role in how we perceive and think about ourselves and the world around us. If you were to substitute the news for motivational/ self-development videos every morning, your thinking would change drastically. This is only one of the many ways that we can reprogram our minds. If you would like to take this a step further, think about the music you listen to. Music has a major impact on many of us; turning on our favourite song throughout the day can drastically alter our state of mind. The messages we receive through music can have a major impact on what we think about and how we perceive ourselves and the world around us. Knowing this, it would be beneficial to screen the music we listen to in order to be certain that the messages we are consciously and subconsciously hearing, which become our thoughts, have a positive message. This sounds a lot more difficult than it is; with today's apps like Spotify and Apple Music, curating your own playlists for desired moods has been made easy.

A lot of music sends messages about making money and being famous so that you can party, drink lots of liquor, do drugs, and degrade women. Most of the music that the millennial generation has been listening to for over a decade now has sent the message that happiness comes from money and power, which simply is not true. These messages are toxic, especially when they are listened to daily. Many of the people that have sent these messages have ended up in rehab, bankrupt, or divorced. You are the consumer, and you get to choose what you listen to, so stop listening to messages that define success in a way that is not realistic, and will not lead to fulfillment or true happiness. It can be a lot of fun to design playlists based on lyrics that allow you to achieve your desired state of mind. Whether it is at the gym, on a walk, or in the car, you can achieve a state of mind that will benefit you the most in that situation if you know what type of message the songs are feeding your conscious and subconscious mind. This is a great way to program your mind for a better way of thinking. As we like to say, one thought at a time; you are either getting better or getting worse; you are either closer to becoming your best self or you are falling further off course from living your most fulfilled life. Train your thoughts, become aware, and you will feel better every day.

We are all going to be ignorant about certain things, and that is just the way it is; but, in our opinion, how our marvelous minds work should not be something any of us are ignorant towards. We all wonder why our life is the way it is. Why we do not have everything we want. Why we are not happy and enjoying our lives. Well, by filling our mind with junk noise on a daily, if not hourly, basis, we are setting ourselves up for failure. Here is a suggestion that will set you on a path towards fulfillment: instead of watching the news or using social media, turn off the noise and use your imagination. Dream of all the things you want in this world, and embed them so deep in your subconscious that you can feel and taste them. If you did this for all of ten minutes a day while everyone else is watching the news or glued to their phone, you would see a massive change in your life, so the only question is: will you do it?

The longer you have had a bad habit or a set of negative beliefs, the harder it will be to replace them with something positive that will bring you joy, gratitude, and love. You must believe in the habits you want to manifest in your life. If you are asking yourself what some of the good habits you should develop are, look towards the people you admire and ask, "What are the attributes I admire about this person?" You should also ask the opposite question to develop a list of things you do not admire about the people that you would never want to be like. Then, take action and act like the person you admire, when you catch yourself acting in a way that is not in accordance with who you want to be, do not put yourself down, acknowledge the fact that you were able to observe your old or negative pattern/paradigm, and at that moment start thinking and acting the way you want. The transformation is going to be so impactful that one day you will look in the mirror and you will not recognize the person looking back at you.

Rx: In a general sense, it only takes about two weeks to reprogram your mind, so over the next two weeks make a conscious choice to replace one or two bad habits with new productive habits. Write down the habits you want to change, and the habits you want to replace them with, then go ahead and commit to the change over the next two weeks, and remember it will take conscious awareness over the first two weeks to stop yourself from acting on bad habits and replace them with good habits. After two weeks, it will take less and less conscious awareness to act on good habits because you will have reprogrammed your mind to act on the new and productive habits you have written down for yourself. Never focus on changing more than one or two habits at a time. Remember the two week rule for changing habits is not a perfect science, and it may take longer to change a habit if it is one that you have had for a very long time.

HABIT HACKS

Piggybacking:
Working towards goals that are authentic to your values and what you truly want will not require willpower; however, it will require some level of conscious effort by changing your habits. Changing your habits can be made easier by using a hack called piggybacking. For example, if you are tired of being on your phone at home when you are with your family because you find yourself unable to be present, you can piggyback off of a habit that most of us already have. Most of us place our wallet and keys in the exact same place when we get home each day. All you have to do is piggyback off of this habit and place your phone with your wallet and keys, allowing you to be more present with your family.

This may sound too easy, but we all have habits already, and so by simply stacking new habits on top of old ones, change will be easier. People often think change needs to be large in order to see great results. We often think of the idea "go big or go home;" but this is just another misconstrued idea used to make us feel bad about ourselves. Remember, that the little things in life matter, and that the little things add up. Using the piggybacking method to stack new habits on top of old ones is an efficient way to create the life you want to live.

Triggers:

You can set up triggers to help yourself trick your mind into developing good habits. Our mind plays tricks on us all the time. It is programmed to keep us alive, and so our mind generally tries to keep us out of any pain. Unfortunately, as we know, great things do not come from comfort zones, which means that you have to become comfortable being uncomfortable.

If you know your mind will find a way to distract you from working out in the morning, but you know exercising is the best thing you can do for yourself, then set up your gym clothes the night before, put them in the first place you look every morning, and do not hesitate to put them on straight out of bed in the morning. You would literally have to decide to choose something else to wear instead. This triggers you to put on your gym clothes, which as we all know needs to be the first step in getting ready to exercise. Sometimes just taking the first step is all you need to take action. It is like Newton's law: *An object at rest stays at rest and an object in motion stays in motion with the same speed and in the same direction unless acted upon by an unbalanced force.* Sometimes all we have to do is find our balance and take the first step. Once you are in motion, it would be harder to stop, so why not keep going until you have succeeded in creating a good habit. Without a trigger, the space for struggle in your mind will increase, it will be a battle of willpower and over time, willpower weakens your ability to resist temptation. A trigger takes the willpower out of it; it takes thinking out of the decision-making process and frees your mind to simply take action. Soon, taking action will become your new paradigm.

One of the most powerful triggers that you can set up for yourself is carrying a goal card on your person at all times. If you write down your goal on a card and carry it with you at all times, you are sure to touch it throughout the day, whether on purpose or by accident, which will trigger the thought of your goal. As we know, we become what we think about, and so by triggering the thought of your goal throughout the day, you will be more likely to achieve it.

THE ACCOUNTABILITY MIRROR

The opinion that matters the most in your life is your own. There is nothing more important than the story you tell yourself, and there is no better place to see this story unravel than in front of a mirror. Our own self can be our best friend and also our worst enemy. When you look in the mirror, what do you see? And, better yet, what do you not see? The mirror is a tool we use to judge ourselves; the mirror holds us accountable for our actions, how we look, how we feel, how we think, and these are all things that we can see in ourselves when we look in the mirror. The goal is to be able to look at yourself in the mirror and see yourself for who you truly are and feel happy about who that person is. Unfortunately, many of us do not like what we see. When you know you cheated on your diet, missed your workout, skipped class, called in sick when you weren't, or told a lie, you will later look in the mirror and have to hold yourself accountable, for the only person you cannot lie to will be staring right back at you. Simply put, we are our biggest critic. We are always critiquing ourselves consciously and subconsciously, and so when the time comes to brush our teeth and go to bed, we often have to look in the mirror, and it is at that very moment you will judge yourself and form your narrative or the story of your life. When you look in the mirror, will you feel great about the discipline you showed and the love and energy you spread? Will you feel great about the decisions you made throughout the day? Did you use conscious awareness to reprogram your mind in a way that will benefit your future self? Because if you can look at yourself in the mirror and feel happy about the decisions you made, then you won the day. On the other hand, if you are disappointed with the decisions you made, you will be disappointed in yourself and this will lead you farther and farther away from the person you want to become. Build momentum each day with great decisions that will lead to more positive self-talk, and use the mirror as a tool for self-reflection and awareness. The happier you become with who you see staring back at you, the happier you will be in life.

STOP WITH THE COMPARISONS

> *"I've always thought comparisons were useless and ugly. It is a shortcut to thinking."*
>
> — *Jim Morrison*

Why are we so often caught up in the lives of other people who live hundreds if not thousands of miles away from us? And why is it that we compare ourselves to these same people, hoping and wishing that we could live their lives? Curiosity! It is human nature to be curious, but it can be a destructive behaviour to compare yourself to others. Comparing yourself to someone else, who has different friends and family members, went to different schools, and worked in different jobs than you is of no value. We could go on and on listing all of the differences each human being has when compared to one another, but it becomes clear rather quickly that comparing yourself to another person will not help you become any better; in fact, it often has the opposite effect. You do not, nor will you ever, have anyone else's mind or body to live in other than the one you presently inhabit, so you need not compare yourself to someone so different than you. The only person you need to compare yourself to is who you were yesterday. By comparing your old actions and thoughts to the ones you have now, you will get instant feedback, which will tell you whether you are doing the right things to be better today, and this is ultimately a heightened sense of awareness. If you can shift your focus internally and become aware of the things you need to do to become better, you will find that your old habit of comparing yourself to others was holding you back from becoming the best version of yourself.

> *"I am too busy working on my own grass to notice if anyone else's is greener."*
>
> — *Anonymous*

THE ONLY OPINION YOU NEED TO BELIEVE IS YOUR OWN

> *"To be nobody-but-yourself in a world which is doing its best, night and day, to make you everybody else – means to fight the hardest battle which any human being can fight."*
>
> — *E.E. Cummings*

We are all blessed to be living in this time period; there are more opportunities than anyone could have ever imagined just one or two generations ago, let alone thousands of years ago. With the touch of a screen, we can begin to learn about almost anything in this world; and, with this ease of access to knowledge through technological advancement, everyone has become, or at least thinks they have become, an expert on every topic. We all have an opinion that we think is educated because of the Google search we did three weeks ago, or because of the two Twitter accounts we follow that tweet about a specific issue. It is great to be informed about what is going on in the world, but problems begin to arise when we become passive observers and believe what everyone else is saying instead of forming our own authentic opinions and believing in ourselves.

Both of us were once observers who were caught up in the online world and listened to all of the news feeds; everything from stupid cat videos, to the world's problems. Until one day when we decided we could not take the information overload anymore and that in order for us to find out our *why* and to focus specifically on the things that would make us happy and fulfilled, we would have to turn off the outside noise and start believing the only opinion that matters: our own.

When you make the switch from living in an external world, reacting to everything and everyone, to living an internal life and listening predominantly to what you want, that's when your world will change forever. We understand that it can be difficult to fight the temptation of knowing everything, most of us have the fear of missing out, but by fearing what we are missing out on, we fail to immerse ourselves in the beauty of right NOW. To do this, you have to mute the external noise It is in your control to mute this noise, and so if you do then you can listen to your inner voice and hear your authentic opinions. When you give in to the temptation of external noise, social media and the news outlets, you forget to learn about the most important thing there is, and that is yourself. It is from silence that you make sense of yourself, your purpose, your dreams, and your goals; so, in order to make sense of these things, you must turn off the outside noise and begin to use the silence and the time alone to make sense of yourself. It is from this silence that you will find the answers to your questions.

Be Careful Who You Listen To – The Poem

Everyone's got one, and they all think they're right
But the only one you should believe is the one you hear at night
Listen to all but believe only your own
For other people's opinions are often overblown

Be careful who you listen to, most people are driven by ego
Their opinions are full of more trash than a garbage depot
Feel free to listen to the opinions of the wise
But be careful; check your sources, these
days many people are in disguise
Your safest bet is always to listen and
believe in your own opinions
For you are the only soul that truly knows your life missions

THE POWER OF NO OPINION

"Opinions... are agencies of self-immobilization. What writers do should free us up, shake us up. Open avenues of compassion and new interests. Remind us that we might, just might, aspire to become different, and better, than we are. Remind us that we can change"

— *Susan Sontag*

Opinions can be very powerful. They often dictate the way we live. Whether it is our own opinion or someone else's, we are surrounded by constant judgment everywhere we go. We must be careful about the opinions we have and accept as truth. This brings us to the power of having no opinion; in life, we get to choose how we react internally to any situation, and it is this same power that allows us to have no opinion. Act in such a way where you decide not to form opinions or judgments about your fellow man, and you will begin to develop a feeling of peace and freedom within. This is because if you do not judge others you will not be judged, which is the feeling of freedom that allows you to be your most authentic self. By acting as if you didn't hear or see someone say or do something silly, you give yourself the power to form no opinion whatsoever. Have you ever lost something without knowing? Of course you have, but you would not know it, and so you cannot have formed any opinion as to whether this upset you. Try taking this mindset and applying it to the real world. When someone cuts you off in traffic, instead of getting angry or frustrated, imagine that it never happened, for if it never happened, you cannot form an opinion about the driver in front of you, and, therefore, you cannot feel angry or frustrated. From personal experience, we can say that through this practice of having no opinion you not only feel more compassion for others, because you are no longer judging them, but you will also feel less judged yourself. The anxieties that stem from questioning yourself and wanting to please others begins to disappear as you no longer feel judgment from your peers.

The ability to have no opinion is a powerful practice. We currently live in a world that is slowly molding each and every one of us into critics and judges. Because of the information available at our fingertips, it is easy to feel like we know enough information and have seen enough examples of how people are to be able to form opinions and make judgments as to who someone is without even having any interaction with them. Not only are these judgments and opinions not fair to the person in question, as they do not know they are being judged, nor do you have any background information on the person, but these opinions are also not fair to yourself. In forming these opinions of questionable value, you are literally robbing yourself of the ability to be in the present moment. We are called human beings for a reason, because sometimes the best thing you can do for yourself is to simply be; you don't always have to think, especially when it comes to forming opinions about things that are not in your control. To be able to simply *be*, will require an understanding of simple-awareness, which is covered in section five of this book.

By forming opinions, you are missing out on the moment—your moment. You would not let a jerk live in your home, so why are you letting them live in your head? Stop giving up control by handing over your power to external situations. Remember that even when you do not have control of a situation on the outside, you always have control over how you respond on the inside. From this state of mind, you will be able to live your life free from judgment and anxiety, and you will be able to feel your own thoughts flow more freely, as pointless opinions will no longer block you from positive and creative thinking. In the beginning, you may be surprised at the overwhelming number of times each day you catch yourself forming pointless opinions about others, but do not get down on yourself. Each time you catch yourself doing this, instead of getting upset, pat yourself on the back and be proud of yourself for becoming aware that the thoughts you were about to have would have been hurtful to yourself and unfair to the person you would have judged. Celebrate the small victories in not casting judgment because when you don't form pointless opinions, you will have more time to focus on things that are actually important in your life.

MY PARADIGM SHIFT – DAVID PEACOCK

I would like to share with you how I came across this material and how it started changing the paradigms that did not serve me in my life.

I did not grow up in the school of hard knocks, and I never struggled through life. I was never broke and did not come from a broken family. I was never abused in any way, maybe just a little bit mentally, but that is a different story. I grew up in a middle-income earning area. I had a nice and easy childhood with two loving parents that did a lot for my brother and me. I would even say they were a little too soft on us. I did not try very hard through grade school and would do alright with my grades, attaining a low B average. Things would always come pretty easily to me, and I never learned to work hard for the things I really wanted. I have always been disciplined when it came to being healthy and staying in shape, but I was ignorant about a lot of things that I thought I knew or was being told. I was the perfect example of a person in a state of ordinary unconsciousness.

One night, I was out having some drinks with a friend of mine, and I would like to formally thank him, so thank you, Jeff Mann. We were talking about how the current way we live is not how we thought we would be living. There had to be more than spending over half of our waking hours doing something we did not enjoy (I am referring to the nine-to-five obligation). We had a good discussion that night, and when I got home, and I was brushing my teeth getting ready for bed, I saw a message from Jeff, and it was a YouTube clip of Conor McGregor talking about the Law of Attraction. After coming across the Law of Attraction, I felt a little ripped off with what I was taught in school, and how I was told to conform to the norm and that only the lucky ones get to live the abundant life. I am here to tell you that that is not the case. It is not easy getting what you want, but if what you wanted was easy to attain, it would not be worth having. I was fascinated by all of this and decided to look into the Law of Attraction further; it was then that I came across Bob Proctor. This man resonated with me; I was hooked on everything he was saying, so I emailed the Proctor Gallagher Institute and began my journey of self-development. I always knew there had to be more to life than just working a nine-to-five job, going through the motions, and simply existing and now there was...

Subsequently, I received a phone call from a gentleman by the name of Justin Grima, based out of Melbourne, Australia. We talked on the phone discussing what I wanted in life, and he signed me up to become a consultant, facilitating the program *Thinking into Results*. Justin was a huge help in discovering what I wanted to do, and he gave me the push to do it.

In September 2017, I was lost; I was trying to get on the fire department while working for a reputable company across Western Canada. After being introduced to the Law of Attraction and starting the *Thinking into Results* program, in October, I became aware and decided to set many new goals for myself. In February of 2018, Myles and I began to write this book; at the same time,

I also decided to quit my "nine-to-five obligation" to, instead, become a business and life consultant. When I told my family what I was doing, they were worried and a little skeptical because they did not understand. Both my mom and dad would say, "You are still going to become a firefighter, right?" I would say, "Yes," but I knew that my business is all I wanted to pursue. So, I sat down and had a talk with both of them and explained that I was starting my own business and that this was my purpose and passion and went on to explain more about what I have learned. My father was my first client, and I will be honest with you, I did not think he would want to explore the material. What has really shocked me is how much he has taken to it and the questions he has begun to ask me. Not too long ago, he asked how he could get into a deeper state of visualization. It is funny he asked this because his sister, my aunt Christine who is an Integrative Energy Healer, certified clinical Hypnotherapist, and a Shamanic practitioner, and I were talking one night and both agreed my father was the last person we thought would be interested in higher awareness and consciousness. If he can find meaning in this material, anyone can.

The lessons that have changed my paradigms and my life the most so far include the *Impression of Increase*, which taught me how to leave everyone better off. I use this on a day-to-day basis now and it makes me feel so good It is as simple as giving a compliment or a gift out of the blue and expecting nothing in return. My second favourite lesson was *The Terror Barrier*—this lesson is so important and has showed me that when I approach a fear-based wall that gets in the way of taking action towards something I have never done before, to break right through it rather than letting my paradigm talk me into going back to where I am comfortable. On the other side of the fear is freedom; so break through the terror barrier! The third lesson that changed my thinking was *The Environment is but a Looking Glass*. This lesson taught me how to become aware of my self-image and realize that if I want to change my life I need to change my self-image. The self-image is the image you have of yourself in the subconscious mind. The way I am changing my self-image is by visualizing the person I want to become and feeling what that would be like. I suggest you try this for yourself. The last lesson I will tell you about is *Your Infinite Mind,* which showed me how to change my habits and become aware of the fact that I had and still have a lot of habits that I would like to change. Understand that if you do not change the habit with a positive habit, you will replace it with a negative habit. A little piece of advice: change one or two habits at a time or it will become overwhelming. All of the lessons in *Thinking into Results* are powerful, but these are the ones that stood out most for me.

It is amazing just how aware I have become over the last six months. It is really hard to describe the feeling I get from helping people achieve their goals, but I can assure you that it is like nothing I ever felt while working a conventional job. I told you my story in hopes that it will resonate with you. I know there are a lot of people working a job that they do not enjoy and that they feel stuck. But I am telling you, if you are willing to put in the time and effort, you can have whatever it is you want in life; it is not going to be easy, but it will definitely be worth it.

DEVELOP YOUR PASSION & TURN IT INTO YOUR PURPOSE

We all have an artist inside of us. We are all creative in unique ways that make us great. Becoming aware of what makes you unique allows for your inner artist to shine through. You owe it to yourself and the world to become a better artist, and to use your creativity in a positive way, regardless of how that looks for you. Uniqueness exists in all of us, and the moment you believe in that you will free yourself of thinking you have to live up to someone else's expectations. At that moment, your authentic self will emerge and you will find your creativity, passion, and purpose. Once you find these things, never give up, not ever! The only way for your authentic self to live is by persisting your way through any obstacle you encounter. Commit to your purpose, and do not stop until you have reached your goals, then set bigger goals and never stop persisting and insisting on your way to reaching them. Do not be ashamed of wanting more or wanting better than what you have. That does not mean you should take for granted what you have right now, but remember that it is never giving up on your purpose that will allow you to grow into your authentic self and achieve everything you truly desire.

These days it can be very difficult to figure out what you are truly passionate about. This difficulty stems from the infinite menu of things to choose from; our options are nearly limitless and so it becomes overwhelming to the point where we cannot decide on any one thing. This portion of the book is going to teach you how to discover your passion and turn that passion into your purpose in the next twenty minutes. Even if you have found your passion already, we suggest giving this a try, just to make sure the path you are on is the one you truly desire. The first thing you are going to do is write down fifteen to twenty things that interest you. This shouldn't be difficult; remember you are choosing from a nearly limitless list. After writing these down, take a moment and look for places where your interests overlap and form patterns. Pattern recognition releases a drop of the neurochemical dopamine, which, as most of us have learned, makes us happy. In developing and cultivating passion, this release of dopamine will be what makes you feel like you are on the right path.

Once you have discovered where your interests overlap, you will have to make it a habit to spend some time learning about these areas. You may have just discovered what you are truly interested in for the first time, and so it is important to take time daily to develop these passions through any of the multiple ways to learn: videos, lectures, or reading. You should spend some time learning the basics of whatever it is you are passionate about, starting with the history and then working your way towards the present. As you spend a little bit of time doing this each day, you give your subconscious mind a chance to form patterns based on the new things you are learning. We know it may sound boring to start with the history, but once you find your passion the history of it is anything but boring. The next step is turning your passion into your purpose, which can be taken right now or after taking some time to cultivate your passion; regardless, the next step is to write down ten global problems that you would like to see solved. Not personal problems but, rather, global problems. Passion on its own is inherently selfish, and that is why to create purpose you must connect your passion to global problems. The place in which your passion intersects with something on your list of problems is where you will find your purpose. Finally write two to three sentences that describe your purpose.

We have broken this process down for you and listed the steps below:

Step 1: List fifteen to twenty areas that interest you.

Step 2: Look for a connection among three or four of these areas.

Step 3: List ten global problems that you would like to see solved.

Step 4: Connect the three or four areas that you are passionate about to a global problem.

Step 5: Write down your purpose, and explain why it is so meaningful to you.

Step 6: Begin learning and developing skills in your area of passion to become part of a global solution.

PASSIONS

- _____
- _____
- _____
- _____
- _____

- _____
- _____
- _____
- _____
- _____
- _____
- _____
- _____
- _____
- _____
- _____
- _____
- _____
- _____
- _____

PROBLEMS

- _____
- _____
- _____
- _____
- _____
- _____
- _____
- _____
- _____
- _____
- _____
- _____
- _____
- _____
- _____

- _____
- _____
- _____
- _____
- _____

MY PURPOSE....

_____

_____

_____

_____

_____

_____

_____

_____

_____

_____

WHAT GIVES YOUR LIFE MEANING?

"He who has a why to live, can bear with almost any how"

— *Victor Frankl*

Truer words have rarely, if ever, been spoken. Victor Frankl is not only a neurologist, psychiatrist, and author but he is also a survivor of the Auschwitz concentration camp. As Frankl points out in his book *Man's Search for Meaning,* many prisoners gave up on their futures, as they saw no meaning for their existence anymore, which ultimately led to their mental demise before their physical death. Frankl was one of the rare men who found meaning in his struggle; he knew that decisions mattered more than conditions, even when those conditions were possibly the most unbearable in human history. With a strong enough *why* to live, Frankl was able to find meaning in his struggle—he was not one to give up, nor did he accept his fate based on his conditions. Frankl understood what much of Stoic philosophy is based upon, which is that you may not have any control over your external environment or situation, but you do have power and control over your mind. You are never completely in control of your physical body; like Frankl, your physical body could be put in a prison, but this does not mean you lose control over your mind. You always have complete control over how you react and respond to your external situation. When you grasp this concept, you will not allow events outside of your control to affect your emotional state, and, as a result, you will become mentally stronger than the person who allows events outside of their control to cause them stress. Frankl's ability to ensure his situation did not overtake his mind is what gave him the strength to keep his meaning for living alive.

"Ever more people today have the means to live, but no meaning to live for"

— *Victor Frankl*

Today, many of us do not have to bear anything even remotely similar to the struggle that Victor Frankl and his fellow prisoners encountered. Statistically, we have more access to the things that we need to survive. Food, water, and shelter are much easier to acquire, and most of us have everything we need; in a situation where all of your physical needs are met, you can get caught in the existential vacuum of boredom. You must fight to create meaning in your life, otherwise, like the majority of people today, you will find yourself lying on the couch on a Sunday afternoon feeling bored. It is easy to go through life taking the directions of others, following all of the rules, and living a life that you know is safe. But why tiptoe through life to arrive safely at death? This life that you are experiencing can be dull and depressing or it can be exciting and full of love and gratitude. But it is a choice, a choice that you, and only you, can make. The good news is that no one else has the right to determine how you experience your life. With that being said, we urge you to choose a life of higher consciousness because this is where you will find meaning.

The challenge we have presented to you is to search for the reasons why you will take action. Why are you going to do this? Why are you going to take risks? Why are you going to be the best version of yourself? Is it for your family and friends? Is it for society; is it for your legacy? Whatever it is that your "why" ends up being, it has to be important, and it has to be bigger than yourself. Your "why" will give you the strength you need to push towards becoming the person you want to be and will help you achieve the goals that you have set for yourself.

If you do not develop your why, then you are more than likely to experience the effects of burnout along your journey. Burnout is simply what happens to you when you are pushing towards something too hard for too long, with a lack of purpose or meaning. We have all been there; it happens to the best of us. But wouldn't it be better to feel as if you were being pulled towards your goals instead of constantly pushing? It has been proven that someone who uses willpower to achieve goals, ends up exhausting themselves and, as a result, becomes more likely to give up or fail in their process. However, when someone feels like they are being pulled towards their goals, they will feel much more energy and see things more clearly, and they will ultimately be able to reach their goals faster and will feel as though they have lots of energy and motivation left in their tank to achieve new goals. The difference is in your purpose: why do you do what you do? What is your why?

Meaning - The Poem

If you can remain focused and suffer for your purpose
Your efforts will one day shine through on the surface
There is nothing greater than what gives your life meaning
It's the burning desire inside of you that leaves you beaming
Yet, most people never discover why they do what they do
Instead, they suffer until the end, without even a clue
They simply aren't aware that things could be different
They just sit around in unconsciousness acting ignorant
You don't know what you don't know, this is true
That's why it's up to you to change your point of view
You must look at things from an objective perspective
If you want to awaken to your true life objectives

WHAT ARE YOUR DREAMS?

"The only thing worse than being blind is having sight but no vision"

— *Helen Keller*

This part of the book is going to make you aware of your dreams. Then in the very next section, Section 4: Take Action, we are going to make you aware that whatever your dream is it can be attained.

What we want you to do is write out a detailed description of the life you want to live. Write it in as much detail as possible, so that if a stranger were reading it, they would hold the same picture you hold in your mind. We suggest going after the big vision, not something you have done or think you can do, but something that you could only imagine. Write about how you spend your days, your dream career, and the exact amount of money you want to earn, the relationships you want to have with your partner, children, friends, and family. Write about your dream home or homes, the type of vehicles you want, and the places you want to travel to. Get really descriptive with however it is you want your life to look like in two, five, or ten years from now. Write this in the present tense as if you already have it. Start by saying, "I am so happy and grateful to be..."

Most people do not think they are very creative, but everyone is creative. You just have to allow yourself to be vulnerable and let the creative juices flow. So, before you move on to the next section, grab a pen and start writing out your fantasy. You'll be glad you did.

I am so happy and grateful to be...

_____

_____

_____

_____

_____

_____

_____

_____

_____

"Whatever the mind of man can conceive and believe, it can achieve."

— *Napoleon Hill*

SECTION 4

TAKE ACTION

The only three concepts of time that we can perceive (present, future, past) are written in the order of which area we think you should be spending the most of your time and energy on. Spend most of your time in the present, the reason being, the present is the only moment in time that you can be taking action, and taking action is simply laying the foundation for developing the life you want. Without action, none of the thoughts you have about the future can manifest in your life and become a reality.

DISCIPLINE: THE KEY INGREDIENT OF ACTION

Motivation is a very powerful feeling that can be used to propel yourself towards your goals much quicker when you feel it than when you do not, but it is of the utmost importance that you do not rely on feelings of motivation to keep you going on your journey. The successful among us know that motivation comes and goes; it is ever so fleeting. Discipline, however, is something much greater than motivation; discipline is a choice. Discipline is doing something that should be done even when you do not want to. This is where most people will give up, and it is due to a lack of awareness. One must be aware of what it is they truly desire in order to stay disciplined. Without this awareness, how will you know if what you are doing is worth it? If you are not certain whether something is worth it, then it is a foregone conclusion that you will not do it, especially if you do not feel like it. Remember, discipline is doing what needs to be done even when you do not want to, so if you do not know why you are doing something, the chances are pretty high that you will not persist when times get tough. The easiest way to stay disciplined is to create good habits; that way the thinking is taken out of the process and taking action becomes your new paradigm.

"Motivation gets you started, habit keeps you going"

— *Jim Rohn*

Rx: Just do it!

Discipline - The Poem

It's giving yourself a command and following it
When ninety percent of the world would
rather sit idly by and quit
Without discipline, you will take commands from other people
You will be ordered around and made to feel unequal
Yet so many choose this easy path in
which discipline does not exist
If it's hard, it's worth it, make a promise to yourself and persist
Follow your own commands or you will forever feel empty
For you will never become authentic and
life will feel like an assembly
Your decisions, not conditions determine your destiny
Choose to go the extra mile; it's never crowded with jealousy
The easy path will bring you nothing but future struggles within
So make a pact to yourself that your new
best friend will be discipline

JOURNAL YOUR WAY TO AWARENESS

In a world of information overload, we must develop habits that will help us organize our thoughts. Writing seems to be the most effective way of doing this. So, one of the steps in becoming more aware is to write your thoughts down. You will start to see patterns developing in your thoughts, and your mind will start to make connections between these patterns, and that is when you will start to see your authentic self shine through. An action must develop through repetition so that it ultimately becomes a habit.

Action + Repetition = Habit

We encourage you to think about and create your own questions that you can use to hold yourself accountable on a daily basis. Write them down and answer them daily. Make thinking about how you feel a habit, because when your thoughts and your feelings are connected, that is when you will be at peace. By digging beneath the artificial surface, you will find the truths about yourself, because at this level of increased awareness you are able to service and silence your egotistic mind. Journaling is a great way to develop awareness of your authentic beliefs, goals, and values; as you write things down, you will see patterns start to form and you will begin to make connections. Develop the routine of writing things down and you will have begun the process of developing beliefs that lead to habits of excellence.

"We are what we repeatedly do. Excellence, then is not an act but a habit"

— Aristotle

Below, we have provided you with a set of three questions for morning journaling and three questions for nightly journaling. Feel free to use these to get started on your new habit.

Morning Journal Questions

- What are three or more things I am grateful for?
- What is the single most important thing I can do or say today?
- Will I react or respond today? Will I be in control of the day or let the day control me?

Nightly Journal Questions

- What went well or better than expected today?
- What can I do to be one percent better tomorrow?
- What are three or more goal-achieving activities that I will complete tomorrow?

After answering these questions in your journal, we suggest picking and rating five areas of your life that you feel are most important to you and rating them on a scale from one to ten, based on how you feel now or felt during the day. You should determine the five most important areas of your life for yourself; however, listed below are the areas that we have found to be important in our own lives and have provided them to you as suggestions.

- Motivation   /10
- Health & Fitness   /10
- Mission/Career Progression   /10
- Love/Connection   /10
- Conscious Awareness   /10

This habit of journaling will only take you about fifteen minutes, and it will increase your awareness and consciousness in so many ways. This type of reflection allows you to turn your thoughts inward, opening up your thoughts and ideas to grow in a space where you will soon start to develop patterns and connections that you have never seen before. We live in a rapidly growing external world, and so it is important for us to etch out some time in our busy lives to slow things down and direct our awareness inwards to make sure that we are finding joy and fulfillment in our daily lives.

Write, Write, Write It Down - The Poem

We should not only write because we have something to say
We should write to figure out what we want to say
If you are not already a writer, you will be shocked to learn
That once your fingers start typing your brain begins to churn
You will realize that you no longer have nothing to express
Instead you will discover the many things
you have tried to suppress
It takes vulnerability to express what
you are thinking and feeling
But it is only from this place that you will feel yourself healing
If you do only one thing for yourself today make it writing
Make it a habit to let your words flow, trust
me the results will be exciting

THE FOUR W'S

To take powerful and purposeful action, you will need to know your four W's: Who you are; What makes you authentic; Why you will work to make your life fulfilling; and When you will do it. The only one that we can help you answer is when: the answer should always be right NOW. Many of us have answers to these questions, but, unfortunately, for most of us these answers have come from external environments that we do not control: the media, strangers, or friends and family. Although we may respect the opinions and ideas of our external environment, we must not forget that the answers to the four W's need to come from within ourselves if we wish to become more authentic and take purposeful action. Our external environment often influences the answers to all four W's, but we as capable human beings have the will to choose how we react and think in any situation, which means we all have the power to shape our own answers.

> *"We have the power to hold no opinion about a thing and to not let it upset our state of mind, for things have no natural power to shape our judgments"*
>
> — *Marcus Aurelius.*

When we realize we have the power to control how we think and react to everything, it gives us a sense of peace in knowing that regardless of what happens to us in life, good or bad, we have the power to have no opinion. We have the power to let it go and not let it distort our judgment. In harnessing this power for yourself, you will be able to answer the four W's authentically.

Who are you?

_____

_____

_____

What makes you authentic?

_____

_____

_____

Why will you work to make your life fulfilling?

_____

_____

_____

When are you going to do it?

• NOW

TRUST THE PROCESS

"It is the journey, not the destination that matters."

— *T.S. Eliot*

A predominant phrase that all hard-working and successful leaders around the globe understand is "Trust the Process." When you begin trusting the process, you begin loving the process, and it will be in the actions you take that you find fulfillment and happiness in everyday life. For those who have not yet discovered what it is that they are passionate about and want to personally grow towards, it will be hard to understand that you can live the best day of your life over and over again simply because the journey is filled with meaning. Most people look at days like Christmas or their birthday as the best day of the year; others look forward to and feel happier when it is the weekend. If you are one of these people, we challenge you to find what you are passionate about, or, if you have given up on your dreams and passions in the past, revisit them and begin formulating a plan to spend more of your time doing these things. If you do not trust and love your daily process, then it is time to make a radical change. Whether you have to quit your job, break up with your partner, or move to a new city, if you are not in love with your daily process, you will never be able to trust that it will bring you the things you truly desire. Life is too short not to trust and love the process, so do whatever it takes to find a process that is authentic to you, and then find a way to do it every day, and do not let anyone or anything hold you back.

*"Live your life each day as you would climb a mountain.
An occasional glance toward the summit keeps the goal in
mind, but many beautiful scenes are to be observed from
each new vantage point. Climb slowly, steadily, enjoying
each passing moment; and the view from the summit will
serve as a fitting climax for the journey."*

— *Harold V. Melchert*

ASK WHAT, NOT WHY...

When you ask "why" you are projecting feelings of the past into
the present moment. *Why* most often does not solve a problem—it
actually just reminds you there is one. Someone who asks *why* too
often will become lost in past emotions and not be able to move
forward and accomplish any task or break through any barriers.
The person who asks themselves "what" will figure out the action
that must be taken next to solve the problem or to improve upon
already developed areas of their life. *What* questions will get you
to take action. Without action, reflection is pointless.

Action + Reflection = Awareness

While both questions offer an opportunity to become aware,
someone who is interested in becoming successful in raising their
level of awareness, should be asking a lot more *what* questions
than *why* questions. In a study done by Tasha Eurich, the author
of the book *Insights,* she found fifty of what she calls "Awareness
Unicorns;" these are people who have passed multiple tests proving
that they are indeed the most aware people, and so they could be
studied to learn what makes them more aware than their peers. In
reading the self-reflections/journals of these "Awareness Unicorns,"
the word "what" appeared at a rate of nearly 10:1 over the word
"why." This is because the word "what" will move you toward action

in the future, while the word "why" will take you back to a feeling that you felt in the past. So, the question you must ask yourself is, "Do I want to be a '*what* person' or a '*why* person'?"

Some examples of *why* questions and common answers will be reframed to *what* questions below. Hopefully, through these examples, you will see how asking *why* could lower self-esteem and awareness of what needs to be done. Meanwhile, asking *what* questions can increase your likelihood of action.

Scenario 1: A child does poorly on a school test...

"Why am I not getting higher grades on my tests?"

- I am stupid
- I did not try
- I suck at this subject
- The test was too hard

Reframed as a "what" question...

"What will I do to achieve a higher score on my next test?"

- Listen in class
- Schedule study time
- Ask the teacher questions

Scenario 2: An athlete has a poor performance

"Why did I play so bad?"

- I did not practice enough
- I was not feeling my best
- My competition was just better than me

Reframed as a "what" question...

"What will I do so that I perform better next time I play?"

- I will get back to basics and work on simple mechanics
- I will eat healthier and get more sleep leading up to game day

As you can see, when you ask yourself *why* all you are doing is coming up with reasons from your past as to why you did not achieve what you wanted, meaning you are constantly impressing upon your mind thoughts of the things you did not do. By asking *what* questions, it is clear that you will come up with a plan and take action to further develop your skills to be ready next time. Asking *what* questions will impress upon your thoughts the things you need to be doing to take action and build your skills. Ask yourself *what* and you will persist; ask yourself *why* and you will resist. As we know, it's often a small shift that makes the difference; substitute *what* for *why* and you will experience great results.

IMPRESSION OF INCREASE

The impression of increase is leaving everyone better off no matter the circumstances, whether that is in the grocery store, day-to-day life, or in business. Everyone is good at something, so bring it to their attention and compliment them on it. When you do this, you will not only be helping others but it will also enrich your own life. Doing this creates an energy that will flow through you to the person you are uplifting, and it will make you feel better in the process. Giving should be a habit. It should be a free-flowing action, a part of your habitual behaviour. Willingly give, and graciously receive. Think about when you receive a compliment from someone, is it awkward for you? If it is, then that means it is awkward for you to give a compliment. Most people think they are willingly giving, but in reality they are trading. To give is to let go completely; to trade is to expect something in return. Energy always returns to its source of origination. What you put out always comes back.

A person who understands this would naturally want to send good energy into the universe. Knowing that energy always returns to its original source, would you consciously and deliberately send out bad energy? We do not think you would; however, if your paradigm is controlling the expression of negative energy, it can be automatically triggered by conditions, circumstances, or another person. You automatically react to a situation rather than respond to a situation. When you react, the situation is in control of you, and when you respond, you are in control of the situation. It becomes vitally important for us to be continuously working at changing our old paradigms. By rewriting our program (the mind) to take a moment to think about the situation and then thoughtfully respond, we will experience the benefits of the impression of increase.

Not too long ago, Myles was excited to have a date on a Friday night. Being a golfer turned writer, he spent a lot of time alone, and so to have a date with a beautiful woman was something he was really looking forward to. In preparation for his date, he went out and bought a dozen roses, six of them yellow and six of them red. Later that night, she cancelled and told him she just was not interested anymore. I guess that sums up online dating; a person can lose interest before you even meet them... Anyways, Myles was upset but knew that if she did not want to meet him then it was for the best. But what was he to do with the dozen roses? The next morning, Myles decided he would hand out one rose to a different woman until all the roses were gone. Each of the twelve women was very happy to receive the rose as a gesture of kindness. On this day, Myles acted with the impression of increase in mind—he simply wanted to add value to each of the twelve women the best way he knew how, and as a result of this, he himself reaped the rewards right away. No, he did not end up going on a date and falling in love with one of the strangers he gave a rose to, but he did feel an overwhelming sense of love and happiness that he had never felt before.

You see, Myles could have easily made the choice to throw the roses in the garbage and stay upset that his date cancelled the night before, but instead he used the situation to spread love and joy to as many people as possible. When you form the habit of leaving everyone better off and sending good energy to everyone you meet whether they are family, friends, coworkers or random people on the street, regardless of what their attitude is towards you, you will be abundantly rewarded. This is what the impression of increase is all about. We know it will be tough to see how you are going to benefit from helping a person you do not know and may never see again, but understand that it will come back to you. The person or situation that you give good energy to may never be able to directly help you in return. The good energy you receive in return for giving it will most likely come back to you in an unexpected way. Realize that we are all an expansion of a universal power, and it is the universe that is going to reward you.

Rx: Go out of your way to make someone else feel special.

Love - The Poem

Love is the antidote to the world's division
Without it we are doomed for an inevitable collision
Luckily, it's in all of us and it's free to share
So stop with the judgments they are really unfair
Love is woven into all of our souls
It's the emotion of all emotions it can't be controlled
Ours to give and receive it is more
powerful than we can conceive
Together united by love there is nothing we can't achieve
Connections so strong peace is no longer a figment
But a reality just ahead in the distant

COMMON DENOMINATOR OF SUCCESS

"The common denominator of success; the secret of success that every person who has ever been successful knows, lies in the fact that they formed that habit of doing the things failures don't like to do."

— *Albert E.N. Gray*

It is not that successful people enjoy doing the things that unsuccessful people do not like to do, but they know that doing a small disliked task will pay great dividends down the road on the way to achieving their goal. The secret Mr. Gray was trying to discover was not only what people did but also what made them do it. Now, think about that statement for a second. What makes people do the things they do not enjoy doing? It is their goals, it is their dreams, and it is that burning desire that gets them out of bed before their alarm clock goes off. What is your burning desire? What is your purpose? What keeps you motivated to stay disciplined in whatever it is you have to do? Dr. Kenneth Blanchard says, *"There's a difference between interest and commitment. When you're interested in doing something, you do it when it's convenient. When you're committed to something, you except no excuses, only results.".*" The person that will do whatever it takes to achieve their goal will see it manifest in reality in due time.

PUSH HARDER

"I think awareness is probably the most important thing towards becoming champion"

— *Billie Jean King*

It was 6:00 a.m. in the middle of winter, and Myles was starting off his morning how he usually does, with thirty minutes of high-intensity interval training on the stationary bike in his cold, dark basement. He was watching a motivational video to prime his mind for a successful day, when Myles' mom, Barb came into the home gym. She sometimes likes to walk on the treadmill before she goes to her office job. She asked him to turn off what he was watching as she wanted nothing to do with it. So, he did what any good person would do, and gave her the remote as he switched over what he was watching onto his phone and plugged in his headphones. She proceeded to flick channels back and forth between home renovation shows and the morning news, and that is when the influencer in him spoke up and said, "If you want to push harder, maybe you should turn this nonsense off and listen to what I was watching," to which she responded, "why would I want to push harder?" Myles was taken back and nearly fell off his bike, even though it is stationary. Barb is a loving, caring person who would do anything for her kids. It's just that she had never learned to work towards what is best for her. When she responded to him , "Why would I want to push harder?" Myles knew it was on him to educate her and many others on the reasons why it is so important to work hard and on how to find the drive needed to push harder every day. If you do not push hard, you will not change; if you do not change, you will not grow; if you do not grow, you will not become your authentic self. PUSH HARDER! Because if it is hard, it is worth it.

Rx: Anytime you need an extra push to get you through a situation, remember the worst times you have ever gone through and use that pain to motivate you to push harder than you ever thought possible.

> *"It is not the critic who counts; not the man who points out*
> *how the strong man stumbles, or where the doer of deeds*
> *could have done them better. The credit belongs to the*

man who is actually in the arena, whose face is marred by
dust and sweat and blood; who strives valiantly; who errs,
who comes short again and again, because there is no effort
without error and shortcoming; but who does actually
strive to do the deeds; who knows great enthusiasms, the
great devotions; who spends himself in a worthy cause;
who at the best knows in the end the triumph of high
achievement, and who at the worst, if he fails, at least
fails while daring greatly, so that his place shall never be
with those cold and timid souls who neither know victory
nor defeat."

— *Theodore Roosevelt*

MOTIVATE YOURSELF DAILY

Many people make the excuse that they are not motivated enough and that the person, or people, they aspire to be must be naturally motivated and always feel intense passion for their work; how else could they work so hard for so long? Unfortunately, this is a false story that a lot of people tell themselves, which leads to procrastination and, ultimately, inaction. Someone who tells themself this story is always waiting for the right time to get started, and they are always waiting for the moment to feel right; they are awaiting a magical moment of motivation that they can sail away on and ride all the way to the finish line. If we are not the first, let us be the last to tell you that this will never happen. There will never be a perfect moment to get started; you just have to do your best with what you have and where you are. Remember that getting started is the hardest part. It is okay to use the motivation you are feeling to push yourself at the beginning, but do not be surprised if after some time the motivation you feel begins to fade away; it is at the times that your motivation level feels low that you will have to rely on self-discipline.

We often get asked the question, "How do I stay motivated?" The truth is nobody stays motivated, because motivation levels change from minute to minute and day to day. So the question that you need to be asking yourself is, "What will I do daily to feel motivation?" Just like you shower daily to feel clean, you must have a motivational practice in place that will leave you feeling motivated throughout the day. Creating a habit that gives you feelings of motivation is the most important thing you can do if you want to "stay motivated."

We suggest that you make a list of the things that make you feel motivated or energized; from this list, pick one or two things that you know will make you feel better after having accomplished them. These things can be mental (reading, writing, conversing, listening to/watching motivational videos), physical (any type of exercise: strength, cardio, stretching, yoga), or spiritual (meditation, visualization, praying)—it doesn't matter what action you take as long as it leaves you feeling motivated and recharged. Be sure to make it a habit to practice these things daily. Just like sweeping a floor, which you have to do daily to keep it clean and free of dust, your level of motivation will also be directly affected by the amount of time and effort you put into it daily. If you forget to sweep the floor, it will end up dirty; forget a few times, and it just becomes filthy. When the floor is filthy, it takes a lot longer to clean than when it is dusty, just like it is a lot harder to clear your mind of negativity and begin to feel motivated again if you have let the negativity pile up for too long.

Rx: Allocate time to watch/listen to material that motivates you.

BETTER EVERYDAY

"Success is the progressive realization of a worthy ideal"
— *Earl Nightingale*

Standing at the bottom of a mountain while staring up at the top can be overwhelming. This is because when you look at the big picture, you can overwhelm yourself with the multitude of future actions that you will need to take. You will also see how long it will take and that there will likely be some failures along the way. If you look at a goal in this way, chances are you will not get started let alone reach your goal. The best way to overcome this trap of looking at the top of the mountain is to focus on the step in front of you—this is known as chunking. Chunking is exactly what it sounds like. A way of chunking to reach your goals is to chunk your long-term goal into smaller short-term pieces, and then chunk the short-term goals into even smaller daily pieces. Once you have formed daily goals, with an emphasis on reaching your long-term goals, you will be on your path to success. In achieving your daily goals, something amazing will begin to happen: you will start to develop momentum. This momentum will help you reach your goals more efficiently than you may have once thought you could have. This momentum will continue to build as long as you continue to set and complete your daily goals. If you persist day after day, you will soon find yourself at the top of the mountain saying, "I did it!"

Unfortunately, many people these days want what is at the top of the mountain right now without putting the effort in. Little do they know, if they were actually given what is at the top without first putting in the work, the achievement in and of itself would be empty, and their inner struggles would continue. For this reason alone, you must be passionate about the actions that you take to get to the top. If you are not passionate about the little things that make up the big win, then it is unlikely you will have the discipline required to make the slow and steady climb to the top. This is why it is so important to love what you do. Knowing that the end result is not going to change who you are internally, should give you the desire to go after something that you actually love doing. Many successful athletes and artists have said they would still do what they do regardless of whether they were being paid millions of dollars or nothing at all;

these same people will tell you that it is for that very reason that they have become so successful. Without the internal desire for action in what you are doing, it is a lot less likely you will take the amount of action required to become as successful as someone who is passionate about what they do and loves it unconditionally.

It is so important to become aware, because without knowing what you are truly passionate about, you could find yourself stuck in a situation where even if you do succeed, you will not be fulfilled. And, as far as life goes, we cannot think of any greater failure than becoming successful and being unfulfilled. This is why early on in the book you defined what success and fulfillment feel like to you. Do not get lost working towards someone else's definition of success because that will not make you happy. One of our favorite definitions of success comes from the college basketball coach John Gruden: *"Success is peace of mind, which is a direct result of self-satisfaction in knowing you made the effort to do your best to become the best that you are capable of becoming."* This definition of success is the foundation of what it means to be better every day. Even though we have provided you with Coach Gruden's definition of success, we recommend you follow your own definition that you wrote down earlier. If you did not write it down, we suggest you go back now and do that, it is never too late to define success. And the way you define success may very well change over time, so it is never a bad idea to revisit it.

Rx: At the end of each day consciously ask yourself "Am I better than yesterday?" If your answer is "no," do not be distraught, tomorrow is a new opportunity. If you answered "yes," keep on going and ride that momentum.

GROWTH

When you begin to understand how powerful your mind is, you will realize how important it is to sharpen it daily through many of the practices we have outlined for you in this book. We can all have everything we want in life, no matter how big or small it may seem. When we become aware of this truth, we start to realize our own potential and the potential of the world around us.

Our lives are built around internal goals; they are burnt into our minds because humans are goal-seeking organisms. When we were infants, we had goals, and we attracted the assistance we required to achieve our goals, survival being our main goal. We did not have to worry the way we worry once we grow up, we simply attracted the assistance that we needed, if we had not, we would not have survived. Growth and change were the order of the day, from the moment we drew our first breath. To eat, crawl, talk, walk, and run took a lot of effort on our part. We were proud young goal achievers, and each of our accomplishments brought a great deal of joy for a number of people. This creative state should and can be entered and enjoyed every day of our life, even in adulthood. So what do we want to choose as our goals? What will make us curious enough to grow just like we did when we were a child?

"What you get by achieving your goals is not as important as what you become by achieving your goals"

— *Henry David Thoreau*

Without struggle there is no change, and without change there is no growth. Without growth you cannot become your authentic self. Change is a scary word to some people, but the truth is you must change if you want to become authentic. If you are not the person you want to be or think you should be right now, then you will have to change, and there is absolutely no getting around that. *"To do things you have never done before, you have to do things you have never done before."* - Sean Payten. When it comes to change, no truer words have been spoken. How do you expect to become stronger physically without exercise? You would not expect to become smarter without reading, listening, or observing. You wouldn't expect to become more in touch with your spirituality without meditation and visualization. So, why do you expect that one day you will become the person you want to be and live the life you want to live if you are not doing anything to change right now?

The timing will never feel right; there will never be a perfect time to get started on becoming a better version of yourself. You will always be able to find an excuse if you want there to be one, and that is because it is much easier to sit around and do nothing than it is to be courageous and work towards becoming better every day. The person who sits on the couch watching Netflix will never fail, because they never had clear goals in the first place. But the person who challenges themself day after day will most certainly fail. It is through failure that we learn—we learn what not to do, we learn how to develop character, and how to stay calm in the face of adversity, but more than anything, we learn how to become our most authentic self!

Take Your Best Shot – The Poem

It is your responsibility to decide the type of world you live in
The choice is not easy; most will sit by and take life on the chin
If you want to experience a life full of joy and fulfillment,
You will have to do what most won't and
teach yourself to be brilliant
Stop listening to the junk noise and fake news
Even the education system is setting you up to lose
The solution is simple yet most will never give it a try
Because ignorance has become their identity, it's easier to comply
If it's hard, it's worth it, you can't be afraid to fail!
Failure is the surest way to success; it's the only way to prevail
The moments in which you lose will be your greatest lessons
Who would have thought failure would be your greatest weapon?
Don't listen to the critics who tell you you're not worthy

For they have never set foot in the arena; they
are only there to stir up controversy
At least I tried, is more than any critic will ever be able to say
Would you rather live with regrets than
take your best shot every day?
In the end it doesn't matter who knows your name
For you are authentic, which is something
that most can never proclaim

RAZOR'S EDGE

You are only one inch… one step… one idea away from turning onto the boulevard of beauty in your own life. It is often a thin line that separates winners from losers; a line that can be defined as fine as a razor's edge. There is not a big difference between people—there is only a difference in the things they accomplish. One person is just about to start a business, and then another person starts it. One person sees an opportunity, and then someone else acts on it. One student nearly passes the test, the other does pass it, and although there may only be a one mark difference, that one mark was the difference between passing and failing.

Sports history has so many illustrations of the Razor's Edge concept. For example, let us look at the Olympics. Pick any timed sport, the difference between first, second, third, and not being on the podium is very often a tenth of a second. Think about that, one tenth of a second can mean the difference between winning and losing. You may have grown up with the idea that some people have it and some people do not. We want you to understand that this is false! For you are every bit as good or as powerful as anyone you know, see, or hear about. Remember, since the difference is only in the area of accomplishments, you have the ability to vastly improve your results; you have the potential to become even more successful than they are.

Vince Lombardi, the former coach of the Green Bay Packers football team said, "Most games are won or lost in the last two minutes of the first and second half." But, what Lombardi was most remembered for with regard to football's Razor's Edge is the "second effort" concept, which he introduced to his players. In a nutshell, the "second effort" concept meant that when a player was initially defeated by the opposing team, he would always surge forward a second time, with the added thrust of a "second effort." Just imagine the tremendous difference you could create in your own life if you were to adopt this concept. Let us use sales, for example. If you sold an average of eight cars per month but then made the decision and pushed hard for the "second effort" and got to ten sales a month, in the short term it would not seem like a lot, but over an entire year you would sell an additional twenty-four cars. How much of a difference would that make in your life?

Another example of Razor's Edge can be seen in Hollywood. The stand-ins for the main actors and actresses spend much of their time doing grueling work. Near the end of the film, the star will exit his or her trailer and come to the set where they get to shine. These people look similar, dress similar, and even act similar, but there is a big difference is in compensation. The main stars earn millions while the stand-ins earn a fraction of that. Think about that, what makes the difference? Well it is the star that is putting in the extra effort each and every day when no one is watching. Something like waking up an extra hour early every day to study, work, and develop their skills. Imagine they do this every day of the week, over an entire year that is an extra 365 hours spent working on their craft. What can look like a small difference on the micro level can become a big difference on the macro level. The small things are usually the difference between winning and losing, success and failure. As your understanding starts to grow with respect to the concept of Razor's Edge, you will be shocked at how often you see this concept play out in day-to-day life. We urge you to go the extra mile; it's never crowded!

SECTION 5

SIMPLE AWARENESS

It is only through simple-awareness of what *is* that we can be grateful and fulfilled by each moment. We all need to reflect on how we have lived our lives up until this point, and then decide if spending more time being simply-aware of the present moment would be beneficial to our experience. In the present moment you must accept the NOW as it *is* and yourself fully as you *are*; this is the embodiment of *being*.

YOU ALREADY HAVE IT

Whether we want to admit it or not, we live in a consumer-based society where the more materials you own, the more successful and happy you should be. However, do you not find it interesting that regardless of how much someone has, they always want more? It is as if their appetite for materialistic items is insatiable. This type of insatiable appetite for *things* is just as common among the masses as it is among the wealthy, so the next time you tell yourself you would be happier if you had more money, just remember that unless you change the way you think money and things will not make you any happier.

After someone does something they really like to do or gets something they really want to have, their answer to the question, "Is that what you *really* want?" will likely be "nope, not really."

There are two reasons that we have the insatiable desire to always want more. These reasons were brought to our attention by the British philosopher Alan Watts. He argues that the main reason you do not have what you *really* want is because you do not fully know yourself, because you never can. And, the second reason is that you already have it; *it* being what you *really* want.

The desire to have more things and to want to be someone else or want to be somewhere else is a pain that none of us is alone in feeling; at one point or another, we have all wanted to be anyone but ourselves. It just so happens for me, Myles DeBrincat, a substance helped relieve those feelings of not being enough or having enough, and so I let myself believe it was helping me, but it was not. I believe it is necessary to explain the impact that the four words "You already have it," had on my life.

I was addicted to and used cannabis daily for nearly four years. I tried quitting for almost a year with no luck. It was not until I discovered the work of Dr. Gabor Maté that I was able to begin healing. Dr. Maté worked among the largest and most condensed group of addicted drug users in the entire world; Vancouver's Downtown Eastside, the city next door to where both David and I grew up. Dr. Maté brings up an extremely important point that he feels most medical doctors and therapists skip when trying to help someone with an addiction. Dr. Maté says you must not ask, "Why the addiction?" Instead, you must ask, "Why the pain?" He suggests that all addictions stem from pain that can be traced back to childhood trauma, so the only way to effectively assess why you have the addiction is to first ask what is causing your pain. Until you have discovered what your pain is and can face it head on, you will continue to be trapped by your addiction; addiction being *any* behaviour that causes physical, mental, or emotional harm, yet despite this you continue with the action.

I began to ask myself this question over and over, trying to reflect upon my past and understand what pain I was covering up through smoking cannabis. It was just a few days later when I was listening to Alan Watts speak on a YouTube video where I heard the words, "You already have it." At that very moment, I felt chills run down my spine; I knew that what he had said was incredibly profound. At first, I did not connect this back to my pain and my addiction, but as the next couple of days went by, I began to realize that the pain I had been covering up for four years was the pain of not being who I always thought I would grow up to be, combined with the fear of never being able to achieve my goals and escape the situation that I was in. I had just graduated high school, with zero intent on going to college, yet my parents forced me to go anyways—it was either that or move out. For the next four years, I spent my life in a haze, dropping out of college on three separate occasions while going through two major injuries. It was, and always will be, a struggle to deal with the pain of wanting to have more and be more, not just for me but for everybody.

For four long years, the pain I felt from not being the person I always expected to be was dissipated the moment my lips touched the cannabis smoke. All I was doing was simply supressing my feelings of pain in the hopes that they would disappear; they did not, and every time I was sober (the first few minutes in the morning), I would feel this unsettling pain of not having or being enough at my current stage of life, and so I would depend on cannabis to alleviate those thoughts and feelings. This dead end habit finally came to a crashing halt when I heard Alan Watts speak the four most important words I have ever heard in my life: "You already have it." These words kept repeating in my head, and so I knew I had to explore them further and understand why it felt so meaningful to me; luckily I did, because it changed my life. The first question I asked myself is what is this *it* that he speaks of? I came to the conclusion that *it* can refer to two things: firstly, all of us already have the one thing that at the end of our lives we will want more of: time! We already have it, yet most people waste it by consuming their mind with thoughts of the past and the future, as opposed to living in the only frame of time that is real, right *now.* Second, I believe that *it* refers to our higher consciousness, which can only be found through being present in the moment. That being said, it makes sense that we already have *it,* because *it* (our higher consciousness) can be accessed whenever we want, all we have to do is accept our life situation for what it *is,* and live right NOW, thus making us more deeply connected to our self and our environment.

What I learned is that when you become aware that you already have *it,* you win the internal battle against your egoic mind. It is your egoic mind that tells you that you are not good enough or that you do not have enough. Once you silence that part of your mind, which is always longing for more regardless of how much you already have, you will find it easier to simply *be* in the present moment and stay there. If you already have what you really want and need, then why would you want to be anywhere but here in the present moment? Proclaim to yourself: I would not want to be anyone else. I would not want to be anywhere else. Everything you could ever want in order to feel fulfilled you already have, you just have to become aware that you have it.

THE TIME WILL NEVER BE RIGHT

If you are someone who lives for the future by looking forward to events like birthdays, Christmas, vacations, or even weekends, it will be in this very process of looking forward to a time in which you will be happier that is destroying your ability to be happy and fulfilled right NOW. Although having a positive outlook on the future may seem like the right way to live a happy life, we are here to tell you there is a better way, a much deeper, longer lasting, more fulfilling way to live. Alan Watts stated, *"There is no other reality than present reality, so that, even if one were to live for endless ages, to live for the future would be to miss the point everlastingly."* In reading this quote we can become aware of the truth that Watts is trying to make about living for the future in our finite lives. The truth being that there is no other reality than the present reality. We are not suggesting to you that you forget about the future altogether—that would be absurd—we all want to get healthier, have more prosperity, and be wiser, but in order to actually become better in any area of our life we will need to take action in the only reality that exists, the NOW!

Over the past seventy-five years, human beings have begun to spend increasing amounts of time thinking about the past so that they can plan for their future, and less time consumed by what is real, which is the NOW. This may have to do with the increased life span and access to information and resources like never before. The problem with constant thinking in the past and the future is that it leads to inaction. It leads people to believe that there will be a "right time" or a "better time" to do something, a time that is based somewhere in the future. Later almost always means never, so if you are going to take action, you need to do it NOW! You need to stop thinking about when you will do something and just do it.

This concept can be extremely difficult to grasp, especially for those who spend most of their day thinking about a future which in reality does not exist. You should take some time each day to visualize; it is only during this specific time that you should let your mind wander into thoughts of what the future will look like. If you struggle to keep your mind from wandering out of the present and into the future and the past, then it is quite likely you are struggling to find joy, fulfillment, or purpose in your current daily actions. It is likely that you are chasing a number and not a feeling. What we mean by this is you have most likely set a goal of what you want your future to look like but have failed to realize what type of work this future actually requires. For example, it seems that a lot of people have the goal of being rich and famous. Although there is nothing wrong with being either of those things, becoming rich and/or famous requires a lot of specific action, not in the future but right NOW. So, if you want fame and fortune but are not willing to take the actions, you do not really want fame and fortune, because to really want these things you must also *really* want to take the action required to achieve them. This is why we are telling you to stop chasing a number and to start chasing a feeling. Once you find the feeling you are after, nobody can stop you from achieving it.

Action - The Poem

Later almost always means never
So it's now or never or you'll never get better
Rise up to your potential, your greatness within
It's only a matter of time if you have passion
The desire to learn, to grow, and be better every day
Will one day pay off in a major way
Stop watching the clock, instead do what it does
Keep moving, don't stop, and rest assured you'll find your cause
Its happiness, its success, and its glory
They can all be yours if you write your own story
A story of action, hard-work, and persistence
'Til death fight for yourself because this is your only existence

FLOW IN THE NOW

Many of us spend most of our conscious lives in a state of thinking that is either in the past or the future. That is why we want to take you on a journey to the present moment. In this moment, there is no past and there is no future, the only concept of time that is real is right NOW! Think about this... Is the time that has passed us by since the start of this paragraph real or not? Whether it is or it is not, we do not believe the time that has passed is relevant anymore, especially to someone who is in consumed by the present. It is in learning to be simply-aware of the present moment that we open ourselves up to feeling and experiencing the miracles of everyday life. The possibilities of what can be conceived in the mind at any given moment are infinite; in knowing this, you need not be worried about something as finite as time. Time is simply a construct of our imagination; it is as real as religion. When we are submerged in the present moment, we can imagine the infinite. Hopefully this gives you the desire to spend more of your existence in the moment that is right NOW, and less of it bound to psychological time. It is only in the thought of time that problems, fear, and anxiety can arise, for in the present moment, none of these exist.

It is a blessing to be alive and well, breathing freely, thinking freely; so often we overlook the simple things in life that could fill us with a sense of gratitude and ground us in the NOW. When we can focus our attention on the moment instead of the past or future, we open ourselves to an opportunity to enter into a flow state. A flow state (often referred to as "the zone" in sports) is something we have all experienced in life. Think back to a moment where you lost track of time; suddenly, two hours had passed but it felt like twenty minutes. For some, this is found through music or sports; others find this flow state while conversing with a group of like-minded friends. Regardless of how you experience flow, it is safe to assume that all of us would like to spend more of our time doing the thing that put us in this state. In a New York Times review of the book *Flow*, written by Mihaly Csikszentmihalyi, it says "Important... illuminates the way to happiness." Living a fulfilled life comes down to doing what is important to you. When you are acting in accordance with what is important to you, time ceases to exist and you enter into a flow state; this is where you become your most authentic self. If you can, try to remember what activities put you in a flow state, then write them down and make it a priority to do more of what puts you in the flow!

The following activities or actions put me in a state of flow:

- _____
- _____
- _____

WHEN THE INFINITE BECOMES FINITE

As human beings, we hold the power to imagine infinite possibilities and outcomes that may or may not happen. Through our memories, we are able to make predictions as to what we think will happen in the future, and the possibilities are endless. Unfortunately, despite our ability to imagine the infinite, we are ultimately finite beings that all have a dreaded last day looming somewhere in the future. It is this understanding of the finite that exists in all of us that causes a lot of stress and anxiety in today's society. For thousands of years, religion allowed us to believe that there is life after death. This belief gave people something to hold on to when times were tough or when life was coming to an end. By the time the twenty-first century rolled around, religion had been debunked, de-mythed, demystified, and destroyed so many times by so many different sciences and technologies that if you were born after 1980 into a non-religious family, you have most likely been exposed to many reasons throughout your childhood and early adulthood as to why religion is a myth. Unfortunately, those who grew up without something to have faith in often struggle to find purpose and meaning. This lack of faith leads to increased levels of stress and anxiety, owing to the fact that you see no importance in the actions you take, and that is accompanied by the fact that you know life is finite, all of which can be attributed to the problems plaguing society today. It is our job as writers to provide you with the ideas and tools you need to build your own belief system and live a meaningful life. Spirituality and faith no longer need to be associated with religion, and so we encourage anyone and everyone to begin developing and growing their own philosophy of life.

Another great way to get in touch with your spirituality is through meditation, which is discussed in greater detail at the end of this section. Meditation is something that can and will benefit everyone that practices it. The reason why is during meditation your conscious mind slows down and your subconscious mind opens up and becomes more impressionable. This gives you a window of opportunity to form new beliefs and attract new things into your life. Using mantras during meditation is a great way to develop your belief system, whether that includes your beliefs about the world or yourself. The more time you spend meditating, the more at peace and relaxed you will feel. We live in a world of infinite possibilities, which can be stressful to think about. Yet, one day, hopefully far from now, we will become finite; knowing that we can imagine both the infinite and finite is extremely stressful and anxiety causing and so if something as simple as being still and mindful in a dimly lit room for ten minutes could relieve you of that stress and anxiety, the only question you need to ask yourself is, "What will it take to make meditation a habit?"

When the infinite becomes finite, everything is nothing. When the finite becomes infinite, nothing is everything. This means that as you become aware of the infinite possibilities of life but the finite (death) is on the horizon, everything you could have ever done or had becomes nothing. This is a sad way to look at life, but it is a realization that all of us will make either consciously or subconsciously as our time on this earth begins to seem more finite. On the other hand, when you realize that the finite becomes infinite and nothing is everything, you will have become aware that the NOW is and always will be infinite. What was once thought of as finite has become infinite and nothing, not even death, can scare a person who thinks this way, because every moment up until their last breath will be new; this person will have unlocked the power of NOW.

Learning to live and simply *be* in the NOW is one of the most important concepts that anyone could ever become aware of and understand. Remembering that you are going to die is a great way to avoid the trap of thinking you have something to lose; it frees your mind of past and future thinking, which allows for a deeper experience of each and every present moment. One day, we will lose everything we have ever owned and loved because everything is temporary, everything but right NOW. The NOW is such a small unit of time that it cannot be measured. If you try to measure the moment that is right NOW it will pass you by before you can measure it; therefore, the NOW is unmeasurable, the NOW is infinite.

> *"So many people of wealth understand much more about making and saving money, than about using and enjoying it. They fail to live because they are always preparing to live. Instead of earning a living they are mostly earning an earning."*
>
> — *Alan Watts*

Consciousness - The Poem

What is real and what is not
If the future and past consume your thoughts
The only real moment is the one right NOW
In its infinite presence the NOW becomes the how
It is called the present because today is a gift
But most go unopened, that is a mindset that needs to shift
Time is money, but money is not time
Forget about the destination and enjoy the climb
It is easy to feel disconnected in this modern day
So close your eyes, look inside, and you will find your way

BE YOURSELF

When you no longer desire to live anyone else's life other than your own, and you find fulfillment in the place you are in right NOW, you will reveal to yourself the power to transcend what was once limited thinking. The desire to be someone else, somewhere else, takes you out of the moment and limits your thinking. You cannot be anyone other than you, which also means you cannot be somewhere where you are not. Stop trying to be someone else and simply accept who you are and what life is. Repeat to yourself over and over again, *"I wouldn't want to be anyone else; I wouldn't want to be anywhere else."* It is at the moment you believe this statement to be true that you will stop trying to become anyone other than your most authentic self.

In order to become your most authentic self, you will need to spend time being simply-aware. Simple-awareness creates clarity, and, from a clear place, you will be able to determine your true desires—your why, and your purpose. The more time you spend being simply-aware, the more likely it will be that you end up in the places you are meant to be with the people you are meant to be there with. Your dreams are given to you for a reason, no one is given dreams that they are not capable of achieving, so regardless of how unlikely it may be to achieve them, we are here to tell you that you can, and you will. It will not be easy. It will be very hard, but it will be worth it. Without increased time spent being simply-aware, you will be just like everyone else, dreaming about their dreams instead of living them.

YOUR LIFE SITUATION IS NOT YOUR LIFE

What we often consider to be *life* is actually our *life situation*. You may be saying to yourself, "Is there even a difference?" YES, it is the difference between living and existing. Your *life situation* is constructed in your mind based on your past memories and perception of the future. Your *life* is right NOW. If you decide to experience living through your *life situation*, we assure you that you will not find happiness until you have acquired everything you want, and even if you do, which is unlikely to happen, it is doubtful it will ever be enough to be fulfilling, because the human desire is insatiable when you identify with your egoic mind. Your egoic mind exists in the perception of your *life situation*; the ego does not exist in the NOW. Your *life situation* only exists in the biopsychology of your perception of time. This is the way in which our brain processes time based on the past to be able to predict future events. This state of psychological time is where all human problems are created—problems which we would argue are not real and were never real to begin with, not until you made them up in your mind.

Your *life* is right NOW! Do you have a problem right NOW? Not after you finish reading this chapter, not later this month, not when the rent is due, but right NOW? As you read this book, it is not possible for you to have a problem, because in the NOW problems do not exist. That is not to say that emergencies are not real; they are, but that is another subject altogether, which we will cover in a moment. When you become simply-aware of yourself and your surroundings, you enter the NOW and are no longer restricted by time. Time is one of the biggest causes of anxiety and stress in a modern society; we use time as a symbol to describe the past, the beginning, the future, and the end. We often try to describe the NOW by placing a time on it, but in reality, time cannot be described because the NOW continues to change. It can never be slowed down or captured as a moment in time; the NOW is infinite. It is in the moments we spend consumed in the NOW where we surrender our past identities and future fears or hopes. It is in the NOW where we experience real freedom and fulfillment. Most people will wander through life experiencing the NOW only for brief moments. Most people are unaware of this, but these moments are used to escape their life situation. The most common ways people do this is through TV, food, alcohol, drugs, and sex. Even some adrenaline junkies are seeking escape from their life situation by submerging themselves into a situation where if they take their mind off of the NOW for even one second, they could get seriously injured or die. The good news is you do not have to be an adrenaline junky to spend more of your conscious time on this planet consumed by the NOW. Simply realizing that you are not currently present in the moment is a form of being present, by becoming aware that your mind is not consumed by the present moment you are one step closer to being present. As you start to become aware of the importance of the NOW, you will begin to notice your mind transitioning from your life to your life situation all day long. The more time you spend being simply-aware in the NOW, the easier it will become to be present and simply live life.

What we are asking you to do next is to enter a present trace of the NOW (your memories). We are going to ask you to enter a state of reflection that may not be all that comfortable; but, for explaining what the NOW *feels* like, we think seeing it through this lens can make transitioning into it a little bit easier. Remember the last time you were in an emergency. In this emergency, your life situation completely disappeared, and the past and the future could play no role because if they did, you or someone else could have died. In a real emergency, all of your attention is in the NOW, and you snap out of the life situation you were in and you become consumed by life right NOW. That is why some people are able to recall in great detail the sounds, smells, and sights they encountered during an emergency; they were consumed by the moment.

Wouldn't it be great to be able to live in the NOW more often? A state where you could fully take in the sounds, smells, and sights of daily life? We hear it all the time: it is the small things in life that matter. This is very true, but also very misunderstood and difficult to comprehend, especially for someone who spends most of their life in an ordinary unconscious state of mind, consumed by their life situation instead of living their life in the NOW. Your perception of happiness will always be scattered in the former, but in the latter you will not need to try to be happy, for in the NOW happiness will embody your soul. For when you are fully present in the NOW, it is not possible to be unhappy; in the NOW, your problems disappear and you give yourself the ability to find joy in the little things.

*"The truth is that nothing is going to make you happy.
Getting what you want just means you are momentarily
pacified. What's really going on is that some people just
don't want to be happy. Regardless of your situation as
it seems at the moment, you are either going to choose to
be happy or not."*

— *Bryant McGill*

What is Real Happiness - The Poem

Let's start by stating what happiness is not
It's not what most of us have thought
It's not success in terms of money, power, or fame
It's something that will escape you the more you try to claim
It's a word used to describe feelings that language can't do justice
Real happiness needs no words because it's its own substance
Happiness is most often confused for pleasure
Pleasure is external; it's something you can measure
Whereas happiness needs no comparison to another
Real happiness is the moment a newborn
child looks in the eyes of its mother

EMBRACE FEAR, PAIN, AND SORROW IN THE NOW

Facing your fears and your pains head on is much easier said than
done. We are conditioned to run away from fear and pain to separate
ourselves from such feelings, either physically or emotionally. This
makes sense to most of us; if we are afraid of something, we just do
not do it; we simply avoid the places and people that will cause us
to feel fear or pain. This strategy works, but it will never allow you
to overcome your fears. If on the other side of fear is pure bliss and
joy, then by avoiding fear you are avoiding joy. You must realize
that each of us has the sensitivity to feel pleasure, happiness, and

pure bliss ingrained into our DNA through our five senses. This also means that we are able to feel pain, sorrow, and fear. Pleasure and pain, and joy and sorrow are two sides of the same coin. Once the fearful mind, which runs away from everyday terrors, joins the seeking mind that desires a better world, all the illusions of the mind will have been exhausted. In this moment, the mind has seen through all fear and all hope, finding a peace within itself, in a state of simple-awareness beyond thought; this is where your most authentic self shines through, and joy and fulfillment are achieved.

In moments of happiness, joy, and pleasure, most people find it very easy to stay connected to the present moment. It is not often that someone in such a pleasant state of mind stops to think about how happy they are in the moment, they just are. It is not until after the moment has passed, that they will look back on the present trace of the past (memories) in which they will say to themselves, "I enjoyed that." However, when we flip that coin over and we experience fear, pain, and sorrow, our tendency as human beings is to try to separate ourselves from the situation. When a fearful situation arises, we default to telling ourselves how scared we are, the same way when we feel physical pain we tell ourselves how much it hurts. This is our attempt to grab a hold of the past. We use these past memories to compare the feelings of pain and fear back then to right NOW. This strategy is flawed in its nature because comparing the NOW to present traces of the past is unrealistic; by making comparisons, all you are doing is creating more pain and fear. What we must do, then, is not try to run and hide from fear and pain, but instead face it head on and accept it for what it is. This present moment is new, and it is unlike anything we have ever experienced before, and so to separate yourself from it by recalling present traces of the past, you will become rigid in your thinking which will result in an increased intensity of fear, pain, and sorrow.

The human mind is not rigid—it has the ability to absorb the shock of any pain and slowly ease it until all of a sudden you no longer feel it. Absorbing pain and fear is simple when you become simply-aware of the present moment; you must understand that you are the fear and pain. It is not something apart from you, and so to try to fight against it will only cause more pain. Cars have shocks to absorb the bumps on the road; if they did not, they would be rigid, and they would fall apart much more quickly. Imagine your brain as the shocks on a car; it has the ability to absorb the bumps of daily life, as long as you do not tense up and allow your thoughts to become rigid. Just as a human being who physically tenses up before falling will endure more injuries than someone who falls loosely and freely without tension, the person who tenses up during moments of mental fear, pain, and sorrow will feel the hurt more intensely than someone who freely accepts it and continues to be present in their life.

Fear - The Poem

The evidence is false, yet it appears to be real
It's all in your mind which means there is an opportunity to heal
As long as you face it head on with an open mind
Fear will dissolve and you will become one of a kind
You see, fear, pain, and sorrow are not something to avoid
They are just as much a part of you as pleasure and joy
For each moment you experience is vastly new
So accept it fully to end the divide inside of you
Stop running from fear it will only limit your ability to love
For on the other side of fear is everything
you have ever dreamed of

ADDICTED TO THINKING

Whether you already know it or not, thinking is the most addictive thing to do as a human being. Thinking is the most incredible part about being human; we all have the ability to listen in on our thoughts as a conscious observer, yet many of us go through life believing that we are our thoughts. The best-selling author of the *Power of Now,* Eckhart Tolle says, "We are not our thoughts." Yet, most of us are addicted to our thoughts and derive all of our self-identity from the ego. It is a scary idea to disidentify from your thoughts, but only if your ego is in control. As long as you identify with your egoic mind, what you will fear and resist most is your own awakening. To awaken means to leave your self-identification through the past behind, and this is why the majority of the population is still asleep, because they cannot conquer their own fear of the unknown. You will no longer see things as "good" or "bad;" everything just *is.* This frightens the ego because it knows that the NOW has the power to dissolve it.

It does not matter what actions we take on a day-to-day basis, we are almost always thinking, but thinking makes up a very small part of what it means to be conscious. According to neuroscientists, the thoughts you consciously have throughout the day make up only five percent of cognitive activity, while the other ninety-five percent of brain activity goes beyond what you are consciously aware of. This should make you question why most of us form our self-identity through our conscious thought. As we said earlier in the book, to identify yourself from your thoughts would be like predicting the end result of a math test with one hundred questions on it after only answering five of them. Most people will never know who they are without self-identification through the ego because they have never learned how to quiet the conscious five percent of their mind and listen in on the other ninety-five percent of cognitive activity that we are generally unaware of called the subconscious mind.

In understanding this concept that we are not our thoughts, you are likely asking yourself, "How am I supposed to quiet my thinking/conscious mind, and how would that benefit me?" The more difficult part of that question is how to quiet your mind, because it takes practice—most commonly the practice of meditation. Before you brush the idea of meditation away, let us tell you that the feelings we have experienced through meditation are the reason we continue to do it. The goosebumps, the emotional reactions, the heightened sense of awareness, the feeling of just being and, ultimately, the moments of no thoughts whatsoever are all great reasons to meditate. If you have not meditated before reading this, take this as your sign to start. It may be hard to drag yourself into a dark room and sit still for ten to fifteen minutes at first, but you will undoubtedly see benefits, even if you meditate in the simplest way possible. For anyone that has not yet meditated, we recommend you start with a guided meditation, which can be found on YouTube or many different apps on your phone; however, we have provided you with a guided meditation script written by David's aunt Christine that you are about to read. It is important to start with guided meditation the first few times so that you do not end up struggling and white-knuckling your way through your meditation session. You will be more likely to enjoy it if you start with a guided session and then slowly work your way towards silent meditation for longer periods of time.

The research speaks for itself: meditation will increase awareness, reduce stress, increase concentration, increase happiness, and slow aging. So what is stopping most people from taking ten minutes out of their day to increase their overall well-being? It's as simple as making unconscious decisions. The irony is that if the unconscious person were to meditate just once, they would likely see the difference in their ability to make conscious decisions, and meditation would then become a habit.

DEEP RELAXATION CONNECTION TO HEART CENTRE - CHRISTINE BRAIN

We are very grateful to have been able to collaborate with David's aunt, Christine Brain. Christine is clairvoyant and she is a certified Integrative Energy Healer and Yoga Instructor. The techniques and modalities that she has studied include Integrative Energy Healing, Healing Touch, Craniosacral Therapy, Yoga, Guided

Meditation, North American Spirituality, and Shamanism, which have all contributed to the development of her personal style of healing and have proven to be very effective in helping her clients reach their personal health goals. Christine has provided for all of us a beautiful guided meditation that is sure to connect you to your authentic self.

Guided visual meditation allows you to go deep into your inner world and access parts of yourself that have been forgotten, suppressed, or buried deep in the subconscious mind. Bringing your inner world into alignment with your outer world creates inner peace and stillness where all healing happens. You are about to learn the importance of mindfulness, the ability to quiet the mind and how to live in the moment, allowing you to become masters of your life experience!

Meditation is a practice and takes time and effort to perfect. Those that meditate daily have the tool to harness their energy into focusing on what they wish to manifest in their lives. Energy follows thought, what we think about, we create; what we think about ourselves, we become!

I have been meditating for many years and have had times where I was totally devoted to a daily practice and times when I would only meditate once a month in a group. Whatever your level of commitment may be, simply give yourself the time and space to explore, grow, and have an experience. If you fall out for a while, it is okay; when you are ready, you will begin again. The biggest thing is to be gentle with yourself. When you notice your mind wandering, simply bring it back to breath. The ultimate goal is for you to find inner peace and stillness. The benefits are many and the investment only needs to be as little as ten minutes a day.

You may read this to yourself or you may record it and play it back. Your voice has a soothing healing effect on your nervous system, and the vibration of the words play a part in raising your consciousness.

Find a quiet space, preferably away from any distractions such as cell phones, computers, etc. Sit as comfortably as you can with your spine in an erect position. Place your hands gently on your thighs with your index finger and thumb touching, palms facing upward. Allow the wrist to be soft and relaxed. And wear comfortable, loose-fitting clothing.

GUIDED VISUAL MEDITATION SCRIPT:

- Close your eyes, and allow yourself to become simply-aware of your breath
- Stay focused on your breath as you breathe into your belly
- Allow your belly to extend on the inhale and contract on the exhale
- Follow this for 5-10 breaths and then notice how you feel
- Notice how the shoulders begin to soften, notice how the tension starts to leave your body, let go, let go even more
- You may now begin to chant a continuous series of OM, AUM or any other word that has meaning to you 5–10 consecutive times, and notice what happens to your body and your mind
- Feel into the sensations of your body
- Feel into the energy surrounding you. How far out does your energy body reach? Is it tucked in tight or is it expansive and far reaching?
- Keep in mind there is no right or wrong answer; it is your experience
- Soften into the silence around you
- Be in silence
- Release all worry, tension, and thoughts
- Surrender to your highest self, your highest guidance
- Trust in your energy body's intelligence
- Trust in the power and knowledge of your own heart
- Bring your simple-awareness into your heart centre
- Allow your mind to travel down into your heart
- You may visualize a staircase or perhaps a big magical slide
- What does it feel like? Look like? What is here that you are ready to release?

- What have you outgrown? What lessons are here for you to keep, cultivate, or nurture?
- Stay in your heart space and begin to visualize how you would like to see your life evolve, keeping in mind that which you wish or desire to create is in the best interest of all beings in all realms
- Stay here as long as you wish
- If your mind starts to wander, simply bring it back to breath
- When you are ready to return, take in a deep breath,
- Release with a sigh and notice what has changed in you
- Be in gratitude for this space that you have created within
- Know that you can return to this inner peace anytime you wish
- Open your eyes
- Notice what you notice

MUSCLE TENSION RELAXATION

If you are ready to meditate without guidance, we recommend trying two different meditation practices. The first is called, "Muscle Tension Relaxation." For this specific type of meditation, we recommend you sit in a comfortable chair or lie down, as opposed to sitting on the floor cross legged. Begin this session by sending your simple-awareness to your breathing, focus on your breath, both in and out as it begins to slow down. Once you feel yourself begin to relax, it is time to send your simple-awareness to your feet; breathe in, and then breathe out while feeling/thinking to yourself "relax;" repeat for as many breaths as you would like. Next, you will send your simple-awareness to your legs; breathe in, and then breathe out while feeling/thinking to yourself "relax." Next, you will send your simple-awareness to your stomach and lower back; breathe in, and then breathe out while feeling/thinking to yourself "relax." You will continue to do this throughout your body, working your way up towards your eyes. It is up to you how many or how few body parts you want to go through—feel free to keep your simple-awareness on any body part for as many breaths as you like, the more you focus your simple-awareness on one area, the more that area will begin to feel relaxed and light as air. The amount and which areas you focus on are not what matters. What matters is you send your simple-awareness where you want it to go and that you breathe mindfully through that area. Take your time, be mindful, and continue breathing at a pace that is comfortable. As you begin to relax more and more, your thoughts will begin to slow down, at which point you may feel the desire to return to simply being mindful of your breath. If you have something to do after meditating, make sure to set an alarm, as it is quite likely you will become so relaxed you could fall asleep. If you are someone who has trouble falling asleep, this form of meditation could be great to help you get to fall asleep on time.

MANTRA MEDITATION

If you want to try something even easier, then look no further than Mantra Meditation. In this form of meditation, you will start out like you always will, becoming simply-aware of your breathing. Once you feel relaxed, begin to introduce the mantra you would like to impress upon your subconscious mind. In doing this, your mantra will manifest itself as a part of who you are in daily life. The most simple of mantras can be one word, "success," or "gratitude," or "joy." They can also be longer, for example "I am free from the temptation of external pleasure," or "Perfect health is mine, and the law of harmony operates in my body and mind." You can start simple or you can get a little bit more creative, but the most important thing is to create a mantra you believe in and that is meaningful to you—the options are truly limitless. During mantra meditation, you will continue to be simply-aware of your breath throughout, and you will feel/think about your mantra on each out breath, or every other out breath if your mantra is longer than two or three words. If you would like to, you can quietly whisper or mouth the words of your mantra. Make sure to do this slowly and feel each word as it will become impressed deeper and deeper on your subconscious mind.

Do not worry if you find that your mind is still very active during the first few times you meditate. Contrary to popular belief, meditation is not meant to stop your thoughts; it is meant to create a space in which you can objectively observe your thoughts. Through observing your thoughts, you will begin to realize that you are not your thoughts, and your authentic self is found at a depth much deeper than your surface-level thinking.

SECTION 6

THINGS TO BECOME AWARE OF

YOUR MINDSET DETERMINES YOUR ACTIONS

Regardless of how you decide to define success, our hope is that in some ways it will involve becoming the best version of yourself. Without the mindset of becoming better every day, it will be unlikely that you will experience growth in the areas of your life you want it most. People tend to have two mindsets: the fixed mindset and the growth mindset. If you are someone who has a fixed mindset, you will tend to believe that some people are inherently more gifted, intelligent, courageous, or talented than you. If this sounds like you, we challenge you to do one thing in your life, just one that you never thought you could do before, so that you prove to yourself your potential is nearly limitless. It could be fasting for seventy-two hours or it could be as simple as asking someone out that you find attractive and would have never approached in the past. Of course you will feel nervous, even the most courageous people feel nerves, but by doing this single act, which you once thought you would never do, you will open up your mind to the idea that most things in life are not fixed. *"It is your decisions, and not your conditions that determine your destiny." – Tony Robbins.* If you decide to develop a growth mindset, meaning you believe anything can be achieved with effort, we promise you that regardless of whether or not you reach the top of the mountain, you will develop characteristics of the person you always wanted to be and they will last a lifetime.

Unfortunately, a lot of people do not grow because they are afraid that it will alienate them from their friends and loved ones. This may be true, and you may begin to grow apart from some of the people you were once close with, but that is the beauty of it all—you will be growing, and anyone who is not growing, is not worth your time anyway. Stop wasting your time with people who are wasting theirs. This is not to say that you should be a jerk or be rude to your friends and family members who are not growing and trying to be a better version of themselves, it just means that you need to schedule your time with these people more carefully and be aware of their self-limiting beliefs so as not to fall into the trap of thinking you cannot do something just because they do not think it is possible. As anyone with the growth mindset knows, anything we put effort into, we will improve upon. So, when you are listening to a person with a fixed mindset, just remember to take what they are saying with a grain of salt, in one ear and out the other.

It is true for all of us, despite how we think and feel that there is a combination of both the growth and fixed mindset in everybody. The highest performers in the world, regardless of their field of expertise, tend to have growth mindsets, but even the best can at times revert to thoughts that seem to be of a person with more of a fixed mindset. Some of the best golfers in the world who have developed their physical and mental skills through hours of deliberate practice can let their minds slip back to a fixed mindset, especially when under pressure, and this is when you will see a player "choke." This is because they start thinking thoughts such as, "They are better than me, more experienced than me, and so there is no way I can beat them" or "I am not talented enough to win at this level." If the person having these thoughts had developed a stronger growth mindset, then they would not be in danger of having their mind slip into these negative and fixed thoughts. Instead, someone who has worked diligently at developing the growth mindset would stay immersed in the activity in front of them and not be distracted by any wavering thoughts. This is because a developed growth mindset falls in love with the process. The final result is no more important than how they get to it, and so by falling in love with the growth mindset and the process of growth, each action being taken is an opportunity to grow, regardless of the outcome; and, so in the case of the golfer, they need not worry about failure of any kind or whether or not another player is more talented or more experienced than they are. Their only focus needs to be on the next shot they face.

As two people who believe in the growth mindset, we figured it would be important to mention that at birth human babies are the least capable beings on the planet. There are no other beings that are as incapable of taking care of themselves as newborn human beings. Despite this fact, we grow up to be the most consciously aware beings on the planet, and many of us go from being helpless to selfless through the process of growth. If this is not enough proof to get you to believe in the growth mindset, we do not know what will be. We all have the ability to go from helpless to selfless as long as we become aware.

THE SOLUTION TO HUMAN PROBLEMS

Do you remember the three levels of consciousness? If you happened to have forgotten, let us remind you of them: Higher Consciousness, Ordinary Unconsciousness and Deep Unconsciousness. In giving a solution to all human problems, it is of the utmost importance to explain how ordinary unconsciousness can turn into deep unconsciousness, which is the root of all problems in the world today.

Any time the ego is threatened or things do not go the way they were supposed to, an ordinary unconscious person's state of unease can turn into a deeply unconscious state of pain and suffering, which can result in emotional reactions of fear, depression, jealousy, or aggression. It is safe to assume that any and all of the world's violent problems would be solved if a state of deep unconsciousness is never reached. The only way to be certain that you do not reach a deeply unconscious state is to disidentify from your egoic mind which labels things "good" and "bad" and begin to accept the present moment as it *is*. In this state of "is-ness" you will identify yourself with the present moment and nothing more, thus becoming highly conscious. The most logical way of teaching people to do this is to have people find their purpose in life, because a person with a purpose will quickly become aware that living in a state of ordinary unconsciousness where you are consumed by thoughts of the future and the past is not a happy or fulfilling way to live. The person who discovers their purpose will happily awaken to the present moment and become highly conscious so that he or she can live up to his or her potential and live a life of inner peace and fulfillment.

THE AUTHENTICITY ATTACHMENT PARADOX

At the very base of human needs, beyond the physical needs like food, water, and shelter, are the mental needs: authenticity and attachment. The reason authenticity and attachment are a paradox is because the attachment that we so desperately need and crave as infants and children is the barrier for becoming our authentic self. It is only when we reach a certain level of maturity that we begin to be able to take care of ourselves and become aware of what we need to do to become our best self. This is simply because most of us are never afforded the time to learn how to connect with ourselves on a level much deeper than what we all see on the surface. Therefore, to connect with your authentic self, you must be able to separate yourself from the people and society that you once needed and have grown to desire and rely on. You must be willing to go on a self-development journey that will ultimately lead you to purpose, passion, love, and authenticity.

It is so important to consciously silence the noise of daily life so that you can connect to your authentic self. It is important to become authentic before searching for attachment because until you become your authentic self, you will not be able to form authentic attachments. Attachments that lack authenticity are an energy drainer. We have all had, and most of us currently have, relationships with people that are holding us back from being our authentic self. You must choose whether to be loved by these friends or family members and remain the same, or become a better person, a more authentic version of yourself, at the cost of losing those friends or family members. When we are constantly trying to conform and shape ourselves into something that someone else wants, this is when we lose the ability to be authentic. When someone lacks authenticity, it becomes difficult to connect with other people without letting their ideas or experiences form your thoughts and opinions. This is because you are much more impressionable when you do not know who you are and what you believe in.

Becoming your most authentic self is a journey that at times must be taken alone. In society today, it is nearly impossible to be alone—we are always connected unless we intentionally disconnect for a little while. This is where, in our opinion, meditation becomes the gateway to your authentic self. Meditation is a tool that can be used to disconnect from the noise and connect to your authentic self; also known as your higher consciousness.

Each person's journey to authenticity will vary in length of time; it could take weeks, months, or even years. It all depends on how far off the path you have wandered and how deeply you want to search for your truth. That being said, we are not telling you that you must cut yourself off from your friends and family altogether, but that the more time you spend alone, while being aware and reflecting upon your thoughts, feelings, and actions, the closer you will get to your authentic self. There will come a time that you feel ready to reconnect with the external world in a way that you have never been able to before. This is because you will now be authentic and searching for authentic attachments. The attachments you once had may no longer be of any value to you as you are likely to have outgrown a lot of your past relationships. You need not worry, because you will be vibrating on an entirely new level, and, as a result, you will attract the type of people you want and need in your life.

One thing you must always remember is that putting yourself first is anything but selfish. In order to help anyone else, you must first help yourself; hence the reason why every time you get on an airplane, the flight attendant tells you, "In case of an emergency, put your own oxygen mask on first before helping others with theirs." This is because you are no good to help anyone else if you do not help yourself first.

When we come to understand what we truly want in life and what gives us purpose, we will ultimately come to the realization that we are beings that are meant to serve, which is why we do not thrive without human attachment. Once we discover our authentic self, it will become possible to form authentic connections. You will acquire the ability of knowing within the first few moments of an interaction if a person connects with your authenticity and you with theirs. We would be lying if we said when we decided to spend most of our time focused on self-development and authenticity that our circles did not get smaller—they did. On the journey to becoming authentic, you become aware that the term "frenemies" is very real and so you slowly have to stop being around people that do not bring out the side of you that is most authentic. Once you get close to feeling like you are the most authentic version of yourself, new and authentic connections will begin to flourish in your life. Making connections takes a lot of action and reflection, just like becoming authentic does. Do not expect connections to develop if you do not put in the work. For connections to be as authentic as they can, you need to balance your time being alone with your time authentically connecting to others and the environment.

Take off the Mask - The Poem

Why do I wear this mask? When it doesn't even suit me
Is it because I am scared of what life would
feel like without conformity?
If on the other side of fear is freedom
Then how come being authentic feels like treason?
Is it because of the media and how we have been conditioned?
Or is it genetic; is our desire to conform predetermined?
I can't put my finger on the reasons why
All I know is I would rather be myself than comply
I play my own game and live by my own rules
I urge others to do the same, stop playing games created by tools
Write your own story of authenticity and attachment
No longer sit idly by and accept the media's harassment
You deserve better and you are more than worth it
No one can ever take from you your values that are authentic

INTRINSIC VS. EXTRINSIC MOTIVATION

The ideas of both intrinsic and extrinsic motivation have been studied and discussed for decades; yet, there are still no definitive ways to motivate any specific individual or group of people. However, what has been discovered is that people who get most of their motivation intrinsically tend to stay motivated for longer and are more likely to achieve their goals; as opposed to those who look for motivation extrinsically. Today, most people are motivated by extrinsic rewards that the media and society have portrayed as things that will make you happy and successful; these things being money and power. For years now, many of us have been conditioned to think that the life we want to live is one filled with an abundance of materialistic items. When life has no meaning or purpose that goes deeper than the material items you possess or desire, your will to create dissolves and thus begins disintegration. This epidemic that has swept across the world could be partially related to the instant fame and over-glorification of the Kardashian family's lifestyle. However, this epidemic goes far deeper than the Kardashian's. As a society, we have adopted the belief that if someone is great at something and successful in that area, then they should not have to work hard for it. If you are working hard, it could be seen as a sign of weakness because having to work hard at something proves that you are not naturally gifted. This mindset could not be farther from the truth, and, unfortunately, a large portion of our society and media produces content that leads us to believe these fixed mindset ideas, which are extremely toxic to growth and development. We understand that money and fame can be great motivators, but they are ultimately external motivators that will not motivate you enough to take the action needed to grow and develop into your best and most authentic self. The motivation to obtain high levels of success in most cases of high performers has been found to come from within. Let your purpose motivate you, not the idea of a big house and a fancy car.

PAIN VS. PLEASURE

We don't necessarily enjoy being the ones to bring this to your attention, but whatever it is that brings you pleasure, will also bring you pain. You can think of pain and pleasure as two sides of the same coin. Unfortunately, we are living in a society that denies pain. You must stop denying pain if you want to grow. You must become aware of what pains are going to be felt based on what pleasures you partake in. For example, in a relationship, the pleasure can most often be thought of as the sex, and at the time this may feel like love; however, if you and your partner break up, this love turns into hate, which is accompanied by pain. It is important to note that if your love turns to hate, that it was never love at all, because love does not disappear. Love is ever expanding and surrounds each and every one of us at all moments. Love is experienced internally and, therefore, it is a feeling of joy. Joy has been confused for pleasure by our modern society but the truth is that the two differ greatly. Joy is rooted internally, and pleasure can only be acquired externally. So when partaking in an intimate relationship, one must understand that the pleasure will one day turn into pain, based solely on the law of impermanence, which states everything is temporary. Even if you find true love, it will not last forever. One day when either your life ends or your partner's life ends, pain will be there to greet you. Never forget that everything is temporary; it is a good reminder to be grateful for the present moment.

Why is it that we as a society have become slaves to pleasure? Well, it is simply because of our environment; our brains develop based on our environments and the environment we live in today is one in which society spends billions of dollars on marketing to attract people's attention. Unfortunately, in today's "civilized" world where most people work the "nine-to-five obligation," we are either too tired to spend time working on ourselves, or we are unaware of the fact that we are not spending enough time reflecting. This results in an acceptance of pleasure through instant gratification instead of searching for a feeling of lasting inner joy. It is through awareness and self-reflection that we learn which things in life give us internal joy. If you do not take the time to reflect on a regular basis through practices like journaling and meditation, then you will continue to live your life as a prisoner to pleasure and pain, missing out on joy and fulfillment.

We aren't trying to tell you to give up everything external that brings you pleasure; if we were telling you that, we would be telling you to become a monk, which we are not, unless you really want to be, then all the power to you. But, if you are like us and you still want to enjoy some of the external pleasures that life has to offer, just become aware of which pains are associated with which pleasures. Start asking yourself the question, "What pain will I bring upon myself by succumbing to my urge to feel this pleasure?" If it is drugs or alcohol, the answer may be simple, the pain is experienced in burnout, or withdrawal, or a hangover.

Feel free to think deeply about what pains are caused by your pleasures. You may be reading this thinking, "I have many pleasures that do not cause me pain, such as playing football with friends." To which we would say that you have forgotten about the physical stresses/pain that is put on your body. Now, these pains may be "good pains" that allow you to grow stronger and if that is the case, then this is a pleasure that you should feel good about taking part in, as the resulting pain will allow you to become better. As we said at the beginning of the subheading, we are living in a society that denies pain. We do not want you to deny the "good pain." We want you to grow and become your most authentic self and so you must be willing to go through some pain. Make sure that you become aware of which pleasures result in pains that lead to growth and which pleasures result in pains that cause disintegration.

FALSE EVIDENCE APPEARING REAL

Why do we put ourselves through so much misery leading up to things that we are afraid of? Take skydiving for example: You are out with your friends having a couple drinks and someone comes up with the idea that you should all go skydiving tomorrow. Everyone starts to stir with enjoyment; you are all high fiving and feeling pumped up that tomorrow you will be going skydiving. Later that night, while you sit alone in your home, you start thinking to yourself, "Damn, I really hope we are not going skydiving." Now you begin to feel terrified, you toss and turn all night long, barely getting any sleep. You get up in the morning and you do not want to look like a punk, so you show up at the place you and your friends agreed to meet, hoping deep down that no one will show up. Unfortunately for you, everyone is there and ready to go. Now you are starting to sweat. You load up the cars and start driving to the airport. You have got your sunglasses on because you don't want everyone to see how nervous you are. The ride to the airport is a quiet one, which gives you time to think about what is going to happen when you jump out of that plane.

You are now arriving at the airport, and you can see the plane off in the distance. The sweat is pouring, and your heart is beating faster than a hummingbird. The instructors are getting you suited up and you are praying to yourself that someone bails so that you do not have to go through with this. Everyone gets loaded into the plane and you take off. You are now strapped onto a dive instructor, sitting on his lap, and you try to make small talk with the hope that he will make you feel safe; you ask him if he has kids, hoping he will say yes so at least you know he has something to live for. It is almost time to jump. There is a light above the door that is red and it's about to turn green, meaning it is go time. You can barely breathe as the instructor asks you if you are nervous, and you can't help but think to yourself, "Please do not talk to me right now." The plane reaches 14,000 feet and the door opens, you have never seen an open door on a plane in flight and so your fear rises even more. As you stand on the edge looking down, you cannot help but think that this may be the end. The instructor tells you to fold your arms and jump on the count of three. 1... 2... And, suddenly, you are falling; he pushed you out because he knew that on three your natural reaction would have been to grab a hold of something and white knuckle it. You are now soaring through the air screaming at the top of your lungs, but just a few short seconds later you realize that there is absolutely nothing to be afraid of, as a matter of fact what you think to yourself is, "This is the most beautiful thing I have ever experienced," and "Holy shit, I am flying!" It is at this very moment you experience pure bliss.

The point of that story is to show you that fear can ruin your day, it can cause you to lose a night's sleep, and for what? You ended up experiencing absolute bliss. It is either freedom or fear that we succumb to in life. I think it is safe to assume we all desire to live in freedom, yet for some reason the majority of people are living in fear. Fear like most things in life is a habit, and this means fear is a choice. Just like choosing who you hang out with on a Friday night becomes a habit, so is your choice to fear the worst in a situation. Fear is experienced in the past or the future, the only way it enters the NOW is if you let past experiences affect the present moment. If you are fully immersed in the action you are doing, you will enter a flow state; in this state, fear ceases to exist.

> *"Fear is a mental construct that we alone fuel with small thoughts that betray our magnitude"*
>
> — *Brendon Burchard.*

THE LIMITATIONS OF FEAR

The number one cause of failure and regret is fear. Growing up being scared of the unknown has only to do with ignorance of what is real and what is not. It puts doubt and worry in your mind for no valid reason at all. We have to realize that all knowledge is infinitely present in all areas of the universe at all times. So the answer you seek is already there, you just have to become aware of it. An old African proverb states, *"If there is no enemy within, the enemy outside can do us no harm."*

There was once a time when the genetic disposition to feel fear actually saved lives; when wild animals or enemy troops surrounded a village, the instinct of fear is what could save your life. In the majority of the world, that time has long passed us by, which we should be grateful for, but, unfortunately, many of us still carry this inherent fear with us every day and everywhere we go. Danger is real, but fear is not; almost all of the fear we experience today has nothing to do with a threat to our well-being and everything to do with comforting our ego. We are no longer afraid of being eaten alive by wild animals. We are afraid of failing; we are afraid of performing poorly, or being rejected by the people we love and admire. Ninety percent of people are terrified of public speaking, and it is not because of any imminent danger that will threaten their well-being, it is because of their ego. The ego is the part of you that asks questions like, "If I screw up, will everyone laugh?", or "Does this outfit make me look okay? Will the crowd think I am good looking?" These fears are imaginary scenarios made up in our own minds that are of little help to us in terms of doing what needs to be done. Fear has become an emotional weakness, and it is used to protect our emotional comfort. If you are given the opportunity to speak publicly, it is a great opportunity for your voice to be heard; it is not an opportunity that should inspire fear in your mind. You must come to terms with your fears by speaking directly to your ego as you affirm: *I will no longer be held back and play it small. I will no longer put up my guards for fear of failure, as failure is the surest way to success, and so it is through my failures and struggles that I develop the character and mental toughness that will be used to combat fear in all situations. No longer will fear dictate who I am. I will embrace my failures and struggles and become comfortable being uncomfortable.*

It is only after you have pushed yourself to the limit that you will discover their never was a limit. The only limitation you thought you had was created in your mind through fear. Fear is a thought in your own mind. This means you are afraid of your own thoughts, so change the way you think and you will break free from the fears that are holding you back. *"Do the thing you are afraid to do and death of fear is certain" - Ralph Waldo Emerson.* Becoming aware so that you can discover your deepest fears, gives you the power to become your most authentic self. If you don't know your fears, you do not know your weaknesses, and without knowing these things it would be impossible to face them and turn your weaknesses into strengths. The next time fear knocks on the door of your mind, allow faith in all things good to open the door; in doing this, you will be ready to face your fears and come out on the other side of them as a stronger better version of yourself.

CONFORMITY: THE CAUSE OF UNAWARENESS

The majority of most people's decision making involves their egoic mind. These people are unaware that their decisions do not align with their values or represent their authentic self. The ego resides in each and every one of us, some bigger than others, but we all battle it on a daily basis. If you are unaware of your ego it is all too likely that you have already let it become a large part of your self-identity. Ladies, listen for your egoic mind, it can be heard as the voice that whispers in your ear, telling you to dress a certain way and look a certain way. It's not hard to notice the pattern of how women dress and wear makeup to present themselves when they go out on a Saturday night. If an alien species were to invade a bar or a club on a Saturday night they would probably think that most of the women are clones of one another. Our intent is not to put you down with that comment. Our intent is to push you to be authentic. Ask yourself why you spend so much time covering up your base appearance to get ready to "go out." Observe your thoughts… Is it because you have been conditioned by the media and marketers to present yourself in a way they deem appropriate? Our intent is not to offend any women with these words—they are simply meant to awaken you to the truth that each and every one of you is perfect the way you are at your base level of being human, and you do not need to pretend to be something you are not. Be authentic and let your true beauty shine through.

Men need to take a good look inside ourselves as well. Unlike women, men are not usually conditioned to look a certain way, so if aliens invaded that same bar on a Saturday night they would not have too much trouble distinguishing the men from one another; however, if these aliens had a superpower that enabled them to see the "masks" that the men wear on a daily basis, the men in the bar would look even more similar than the women. Most of them would be wearing a "tough guy" mask. These masks are being worn out of the fear of how they would be perceived if they were vulnerable and authentic. Men are conditioned to act a certain way, while women are conditioned to look a certain way. It is a sad reality that society has conditioned us to look and act in certain ways, and what's even sadder is how successful they have been.

Authenticity has been stripped from most people without them even realizing it has happened. Media and marketing has done a great job at making you believe you have chosen to be who you are, but the reality of it is, most people have not been able to free themselves from the prison of self-identification through their thinking and egoic mind. You are not your thoughts; you are much more than that, you are a spiritual being, living in a physical body with an intellect. Unfortunately, Western culture has conditioned us to believe that our thoughts are who we are. This is wrong. Our conscious thoughts only make up five percent of cognitive activity; why would you define yourself based on a proportion of cognitive activity so small? We are not saying thoughts are not important. On the contrary, change the way you think and you can change your life. But to make powerful decisions that lead to actions that align with your authentic values, you must transcend limited thinking into realms of higher consciousness where you become able to tap into your subconscious mind. You must free yourself from the chains that the media and external environment has put on you to drown you in a pool of conformity. Once you are in a state of higher consciousness you will be able to observe your thoughts, which allows you to understand yourself on a deeper level and gives you the ability to choose how you respond to your thoughts. This also transfers over into your daily interactions—if you are in a state of higher consciousness you will be able to observe your thoughts and thoughtfully respond as opposed to reacting with based on your emotions. If you are beginning to understand that you can observe your thoughts, we would like you to ask yourself this question: Am I my thoughts, or am I the observer of my thoughts? If you identify yourself as the observer of your thoughts, you will no longer be satisfied with conforming to the societal norm because you will be connected to your authentic self and you will be operating on a level of higher consciousness.

ARE YOU BUSY OR PRODUCTIVE?

Although filling your life with numerous activities may seem like a great idea to become successful, without awareness the actions you take may not have the intended effect on your life or the others around you. Without awareness, you will not fully understand why you are taking certain actions. There is a big difference between being busy and being productive. The biggest difference being, when you are busy you are only doing something to pass the time, whereas when you are productive you are doing something that is working towards your purpose. Once you realize why you do what you do, you will become a much more productive person. You will no longer linger through life, only existing by filling your day with menial tasks to keep busy; you will now have the passion and burning desire to attack your day with intent and purpose. We could all use a little more productivity in our lives; every now and again ask yourself, "Am I busy, or am I productive?

SECTION 7

LAWS OF THE UNIVERSE

CREATE OR DISINTEGRATE

The universal laws are something that work all the time with every person. There is a basic law of life that says Create or Disintegrate, absolutely nothing stays where it is. When someone says they are comfortable right where they are, they are showing their ignorance to this basic law. You are either moving in one direction or the other. This means if you are not working towards something or bettering yourself in any way, you are disintegrating. We are literally living in an ocean of motion, but you are the one in control of the tides.

Understand that everything in life is an expression of the spirit, and it always favours expansion and fuller expression, never disintegration. All of nature expands and expresses itself in a great way—nature knows no failures. Now, that does not mean you are not going to experience failures in your life situations. You will probably experience many, but you have to understand that failure is a big part of growth, and without failure you will never learn what you need to do to change and become better. Some people think failure causes disintegration, but in reality it is the groundwork for creation.

LAW OF POLARITY

There is a positive and negative effect in everything. In the Chinese philosophy of Yin-Yang, yin is the passive, negative force, and yang is the active, positive force. This philosophy describes that these positive and negative forces are complementary rather than opposing. The two halves only exist because of each other—without the Yin there would be no Yang. When looking at the Taijitu (Yin Yang) symbol you will realize that there are not only two halves that make a whole, but also two dots in each half that represents the opposite. Not only are positive and negative connected, but everything positive will by law have negative attached to it and vice versa; this means that nothing is never completely yin or yang (positive or negative), but instead everything contains both aspects when looked upon at a deep enough level.

Make a habit of looking for the good in all situations, because just like there is bad in all situations there is also good in all situations. If you look at the good, your life experience will be better; you will have better relationships, earn more money, and live a healthier life. If there is something that you perceive as being bad or negative, it is nothing but a challenge that you have attracted into your life, whether it be consciously or subconsciously. Know that if you have a small challenge in front of you and you work your way through it, on the other side of it is a small opportunity for growth. If it is a big challenge, and you work your way through it, on the other side of it is a big opportunity for growth. In any "bad" situation, growth can always be the "good" that you take away from the experience.

LAW OF RELATIVITY

It does not matter what is going on, if you think you are having a bad day, I guarantee it is a good day compared to someone else's. Nothing is good or bad—nothing is big or small as long as you invoke the law of relativity everything just is.

A Taoist story was once told which speaks very clearly to the idea that nothing is inherently good or bad; we make it as such based on our own reactions. Taoism is a religious or philosophical tradition of Chinese origin which emphasizes living in harmony with the Tao. The Tao being the absolute principle underlying the universe, the principle being that everything just *is*.

"When an old farmer's stallion wins a prize at a country show, his neighbour calls round to congratulate him, but the old farmer says, "Who knows what is good and what is bad?" The next day some thieves come and steal his valuable animal. His neighbour comes to commiserate with him, but the old man replies, "Who knows what is good and what is bad?" A few days later the spirited stallion escapes from the thieves and joins a herd of wild mares, leading them back to the farm. The neighbour calls to share the farmer's joy, but the farmer says, "Who knows what is good and what is bad?" The following day, while trying to break in one of the mares, the farmer's son is thrown and fractures his leg. The neighbour calls to share the farmer's sorrow, but the old man's attitude remains the same as before. The following week, the army passes by, forcibly conscripting soldiers for the war, but they do not take the farmer's son because he cannot walk. The neighbour thinks to himself, "Who knows what is good and what is bad?" and realizes that the old farmer must be a Taoist sage.

LAW OF VIBRATION

The Law of Vibration explains that our feelings are actually vibrations, and so whatever we believe, will be expressed in our body and mind as a vibration. If we believe good things, we will send and receive good vibrations; if we believe bad things, we will send and receive bad vibrations. Our beliefs, good or bad, play a big role in the frequency of vibrations we send out to the universe. Ask yourself whether your belief system is helping or hurting you. If it is hurting you, then you know that you have a paradigm that needs to shift.

Nothing rests, everything moves, we are vibrating all the time and we can only attract to us what is in harmonious vibration within ourselves. Science and Theology has taught us that nothing is created or destroyed, it is in one state or another, so imagine a body in a coffin that we consider dead, the soul has moved out of it but it is still vibrating. If you took that body and looked at it through a microscope, you would see it moving. Think, if that body was not vibrating, how would it ever turn to dust? Now that is something to think about.

LAW OF ATTRACTION

This is the secondary law to the Law of Vibration. This is what the book and movie *The Secret* was based off of. The pictures you internalize and bring feeling to will start to move toward you. Think about the people in your life right now; realize that you have attracted them into your life whether you like them or not. Think about your current finances; realize that your finances are the way they are because of the way you think; if you are poor, you have attracted struggle into your life, and if you are rich, you have attracted prosperity into your life. Most people want to blame their conditions for who they are, but the truth is it is because of your paradigm that you are who you are. If you are rich, your habitual thought pattern is that your life is full of abundance, and, as a result it becomes that way. You attract what you think about, so be aware of your thoughts and make sure to shift your paradigm if you are not attracting into your life the people and things that you want.

In order to attract into your life the people and things you truly desire, you will need to feel like you already have what you want. If you can feel it in the palm of your hands as if it is already yours, then you will be vibrating on a frequency that will attract these things into your life. Start with scheduling ten to fifteen minutes of visualization each day, try to see and feel your vision more and more clearly each day. As your vision becomes clear, the universe will begin bringing you what you desire. Remember that the last and most important piece of the Law of Attraction is putting your feelings into actions, and this is when you will be vibrating at the highest frequency.

CAUSE AND EFFECT

Ralph Waldo Emerson said *"this is the law of laws."* Every educational program talks about how behaviour impacts results. We end up going through all kinds of behaviour modification programs but the results do not really change. Behaviour does cause results, but you have got to understand that it is a secondary cause; you have to ask, what is the root cause of the behaviour. Everything you see around you in the world is an effect: your behaviour is an effect; your results are an effect. What we want to do is find out what is the cause of the effect. The cause is your paradigm—it is the ideas that have been locked in your emotional mind. You have to become aware of your paradigms in order to change the effect. Until you dig deeper into the root cause, you will never get the desired effect.

LAW OF PERPETUAL TRANSMUTATION OF ENERGY

Energy is forever moving into form, through form, and back into form. The energy flows in, we give it an image, and we internalize the image in our subconscious mind, and that idea will then move into physical form. Any idea that you hold in your mind, good or bad, that you continually dwell on will begin to appear in the most convenient and appropriate form available. Whether it is a good or bad idea, if you continually dwell on it, it's going to happen. Let's think about it this way, look at the results you are getting in your life right now. Those results are a direct representation of the thoughts you have been dwelling on. If you don't like the result, then you must become consciously aware of your thoughts so that when you come across one you don't like you can say "next" and change it to something you do want. You are probably thinking, how am I supposed to manage my thoughts all day? It takes time and practice but once you get familiar with the concept of objective observation you will be able to stop thinking the thoughts that do not serve you.

LAW OF RHYTHM

Did you know your mind, intellect, physical body, and spirit flow up and down? Some days you don't feel so good and others you feel like a million bucks. Some days you can figure out any challenge, and other days it would take you forever to just figure out one challenge. Understand that when mentally, emotionally, and physically you are at a critical low you will feel like giving up, but do not, because you can find peace in knowing that due to the law of rhythm it's going to get better.

LAW OF GESTATION

We know that when a baby is conceived it takes approximately nine months for it to make its debut on this planet. Think of the conscious mind as the male factor and the subconscious mind as the female factor for spiritual seeds. All seeds or thoughts you have on the conscious level are being imprinted on the subconscious mind and will have an incubation or gestation period.

The goals and dreams you choose to impress on your subconscious mind should have a date attached to them. Understand that if the goal does not happen by the date you selected, then one of two things has happened. Either you did not give enough energy to the seed and so it did not imprint deep enough on the subconscious mind, or you underestimated how long it would take. Do not be discouraged, set a new date and keep going.

LAW OF COMPENSATION

The amount of money you earn will always be in exact ratio with the need for what you do, your ability to do it, and the difficulty in replacing you. Ask yourself if there is a need for what you do. And we would guess there is. Really focus on the second step, your ability to do it, if every day you become better at what you do, even if only by a fraction of a percentage you will be very difficult to replace. You do not get rich by doing certain things, you get rich by doing things a certain way. In the book *Think and Grow Rich*, Napoleon Hill talks about doing more than what you are being paid for. He said *"If you are not willing to do more than what you are paid for, then you will never get paid more for what you are doing."* Really think about that; unfortunately, a lot of people in the workforce today have the belief that they should not have to do something that is not in their job description. This is why some people never grow in a company. It would be like standing in front of a fireplace and saying give me the heat then I will put on the wood, it simply does not work that way.

LAW OF IMPERMANENCE

One of the oldest sayings in the world goes like this… "nothing lasts forever," which also means everything is temporary. Your job, your friends, your family, your house, your car, your dog, your wife, and even this very moment are all temporary. By understanding that this is law, you may be able to find peace more easily in the face of losing loved ones, things you care about, or even time and opportunities. Let the Law of Impermanence motivate you to spend your time fully immersed in the now, free from the fear of loss. Seneca once wrote *"A person who suffers before it is necessary, suffers more than necessary."* By fearing loss you are creating internal suffering before it is necessary. The only way to escape this unnecessary suffering is to accept that nothing lasts forever and to let go of the idea of trying to hold on to things and people. Just remember that everything is temporary and so to fear loss is to suffer prematurely. Do not be like the majority who spend most of their life suffering prematurely; instead, immerse yourself in the moment that is always right NOW and feel the joy that comes along with being present at all times.

Laws of the Universe - The Poem

Most people think of law as authority
Why do we conform to the majority?
The Universe has always worked on law
What we are about to tell you might put you in awe
Your life today has been determined by your thoughts
If you were aware you would probably change a lot
Law is working for every person all of the time
If you are not aware of the laws, you are
committing a universal crime
Now, this crime will not get you in trouble
But if you change your thoughts, your experience will be double.

SECTION 8

WELL BEING

MENTAL HEALTH IN THE TWENTY-FIRST CENTURY

In the last 100 years, we have been conditioned to put on a mask and pretend that everything is just fine, even when our self-talk becomes destructive; we have all been told at one point or another to "suck it up." But, the time for suppressing how you truly feel is over. If you are not around people that allow you to be authentic and express how you feel and who you are at the core of your being, then it is time you find new people to spend your time with. Even if you do not want to meet new people, there are more free online resources than ever before to help you talk through your emotions and gain feelings of clarity. Within the last few years, the "Let's Talk" movement has gained momentum, and we think that that is absolutely fantastic. But, let's be clear about one thing, mental health is not something that only people with diagnosed symptoms or conditions should be concerned about; rather, mental health is the largest problem affecting society today, and it is due to a lack of both awareness and simple-awareness. Someone who lacks awareness lacks the ability to understand what areas they are lacking in; whether this is self-esteem, self-image, self-confidence, or self-talk, if you are not aware, you will not be able to better yourself, and thus you will not be as mentally healthy as you could be. The Old English word *hælth*, of German origin, is related to being whole. Being healthy simply means to be whole, and to be whole, one must connect with their authentic self. Therefore, to become authentic, you must heal.

We are sure some of you are reading this right now thinking, "I don't have a mental health problem," to which we would respond, "Do you have the ability to think?" Because if you are a human being with thoughts, you have a mental health problem. If you have ever thought to yourself that you are not good enough or smart enough, not strong enough, not good looking enough, not rich enough, or not popular enough, you have a mental health problem. We ask you to be honest with yourself as we ask you this next question, "Have you ever felt depressed?" For those of you that answered "yes," thank you for your honesty, to those of you that answered "no," consider these symptoms of depression and then answer the question one more time: feelings of helplessness and hopelessness; loss of interest in daily activities; appetite or weight changes; sleep changes; anger or irritability; loss of energy; self-loathing; or reckless behaviour. We are pretty certain these symptoms are just a part of life, meaning depression is a part of life.

Life is hard for everyone, and everyone's hard is different—we cannot compare what is hard to one person with someone else because as much as you can try to look at a situation from someone else's point of view, you will never be able to feel what it is like to live in that person's mind. Be accepting that what is hard is different for each and every person and instead of judging them, or even worse, telling them to "suck it up," be empathetic and ask questions that will help the person feel like you are trying to understand. The two words that can help make anyone who is feeling down feel better are, "me too." You may not be able to relate to the exact situation someone is going through, but remember, we have all been through hard times and if you care, you can relate, and if you can relate, you can help. This means we can all help be a part of the solution.

SELF-ESTEEM MOVEMENT

This movement that continues to plague society and, more specifically, millennials began sometime in the 1970s and has continued growing into what it has become today, which is a generation of people filled with anxiety and the fear of failure. This happened through no fault of our own (we are both millennials who grew up in households that fostered a false sense of self-esteem); parents, teachers, and society thought it would be a good idea for everyone to "feel good" about themselves, regardless of whether they won or lost. In many cases, at a young age, the score of a game was not kept so that no one's feelings would get hurt, and of course everyone would get a participation medal. What was forgotten at that time was the long-term effect this would have on these children, not only on the child who lost but also on the child who won. Having no decisive winner or loser taught the loser that the outcome did not matter, it also never taught him or her how to deal with losing, which as a by-product, robbed the child of the opportunity to ever use a loss as a learning experience, which is vital in growth and development in any skill. Let's not forget about the winner. The winner learned that the effort he or she put into winning did not matter, and so they would not put in the effort in the future, and just like the loser, who never got to learn how to grow from a loss, the winner never got to learn how to be humble and grateful in victory.

By trying to protect their children, parents, teachers, and coaches ended up doing more harm than good. Insulating them from experiences that would have facilitated growth was detrimental to long-term happiness and success. Unfortunately, this is the case for the majority of millennials in society today, and most of them are not aware and do not understand what has happened to them and how their upbringing has affected who they have become. When you are sheltered from struggle, you never learn how to grow or deal with challenges; you become dependent on those who taught you what you know because you know nothing else. When the time comes and adult responsibilities begin to pile up, a person with high self-esteem built on false confidence will crumble under the pressure of responsibility and feel anxious and stressed. They were never taught the value of awareness and how it could be used to solve problems on their own. This is without a shadow of a doubt one of the most devastating results of the Self-Esteem Movement. We must be able to solve problems and cope on our own, because without these skills we can never become authentic.

THE POWER OF VULNERABILITY

> *"Vulnerability is the birthplace of innovation, creativity, and change."*
>
> — *Brené Brown*

A myth that plagues our society today is that vulnerability is a weakness. Vulnerability is a power, not a weakness. Unfortunately, we all put on masks throughout the day to portray what and who we think others want us to be, and these masks are used to hide our authentic self from the people around us, for we are afraid that if people knew who we really were, and how we really felt, that they would not accept us as we are. This fear of not being accepted for who we are is the reason that we put on a mask every day. This way of living, keeping the real you bottled up and hidden away from the world, and sometimes even yourself, is mentally and emotionally unhealthy and stems from childhood and the way we were raised. As a child, there is nothing scarier than being alone, so to make sure we were not alone we would blend in and become part of a group; the mask begins to form. As a child, it is far too scary to speak up for yourself and for others, regardless of whether or not what is happening is wrong or unethical. So instead of doing the right thing, the child puts on his or her mask without even knowing the repercussions this will have in the future. The repercussions are quite simple: the detachment from oneself begins, and you continue to follow a path in life that leads you further and further away from authenticity, all in the name of attachment, and therein lies the paradox between authenticity and attachment.

To become more vulnerable, you will have to go against the old ways of thinking that you developed since you were a child. Since birth, most of us have been conditioned to desire security, and, as we get older, we desire it more and we use it to cling to what we have. We do this out of fear that the future is not certain, and this is a fear that we are going to have to come to terms with and accept because the future will never be certain. This fear can be traced back to the idea of death being the end of consciousness, which it very well may be, but it also might not be. Nobody truly knows what happens after someone's heart stops beating, but we also do not know what happens before someone's heart starts beating. This being true, why do we not think about the idea that before birth, one is in a similar state as after death? In looking at it this way, the fear of death becomes much more bearable. Seeing as we have all already been in a state of unknowingness/darkness before birth, there is no need to fear what comes after the end of life as we know it, for we have already experienced it at least once, and the first time around wasn't so scary.

The human desire for security tends to increase the closer we get to the end of life, but by clinging to what we are and what we have, we lose our ability to be vulnerable and we will miss out on the opportunity to feel deeply in each moment that passes us by, which is to miss the point of living all together. Alan Watts writes, "To be passing is to live; to remain and continue is to die. Life, change, movement, and insecurity are so many names for the same thing." "Insecurity" is just another word for "life," which means that if you are seeking security, you are not living. To live with vulnerability, you must accept the unknown, and you must stop trying to control what is an unpredictable future. Trying to feel secure in your life, detaches you from being able to immerse yourself in the present moment; it causes you to perceive vulnerability as a weakness because being vulnerable means being willing to take risks, risks that are inherently risky. Life, by definition, inhabits insecurity. Do not fear it, do not fear the unknown either, accept them, make friends with them, and you will be able to live a fulfilled life. For it is the wonder of the unknown that makes life worth living!

As a society, we are still pushing back against vulnerability, even when we know that to be vulnerable is to be courageous. To step into the unknown and to take chances and be yourself is emotionally risky—you could end up hurt; however, you can only experience extreme happiness and joy if you open yourself up to the possibility of extreme hurt. Even once you believe this to be true, it will be difficult to open yourself up if you let past fears and pain scare you from experiencing new things. There is nothing more courageous than being vulnerable, especially in today's society which is filled with people wearing masks to protect their feelings. Unfortunately for these mask wearers, they are not only hiding from their authentic self, but they are also giving up the chance to feel great happiness and great love for the feeling of security.

EMOTIONAL INTELLIGENCE VS. EMOTIONAL AGILITY

Emotional intelligence is your ability to be aware, and, thus, in control of your emotions. As you learn to control your emotions instead of reacting to them, you will be able to respond in a thoughtful way. The downside to this is it does not allow you to fully feel the emotion. Instead, you have to suppress it for the time being so that your response will be thoughtful and not emotional.

"Emotional Agility is the ability to be with your thoughts, emotions, and stories in ways that are compassionate, curious, and courageous and in concord with your values." - Susan David. Emotional agility is a skill built on the foundation of emotional intelligence. In order to be emotionally agile, you have to first be emotionally intelligent. Put more simply, you have to first be aware of the emotions you

are feeling in order to be able to be with them in a compassionate, curious, and courageous way. The ability to control your emotions when you need to is fantastic, but to also be able to later reflect on your emotions and come to an understanding about what caused you to feel a certain way, and why, is priceless.

If someone has a sad or depressed thought, they are likely to think of that thought as bad. Therefore, if the thought is, "I am sad," then you must be bad; on the contrary, a thought on its own is not inherently good or bad. You only think of sadness as a bad thought because you have been conditioned to believe that the only way to be happy is to think happy thoughts all the time. This type of thinking is detrimental to your long-term health and, ironically, your happiness. Suppressing your sad, depressed, frustrated, and angry thoughts will not make them go away. Masking them with unauthentic positive thinking will only make your "bad" feelings manifest even deeper. If we asked you right now not to think about a garden gnome, chances are you would think about a garden gnome. The same goes for emotions. By telling yourself not to be sad, you will simply think about sadness, on either a conscious and subconscious level. Unless you allow yourself to be with and feel each emotion, accept it for what is, and use your awareness to determine the root cause of the emotion so that you can face it head on, you will forever be suppressing emotions that will lead you to feel symptoms of guilt, shame, and depression.

We have all been in a situation that should have made us feel happy, but we just could not feel that way; instead, we felt some type of sadness and so we think to ourselves, "What is wrong with me, why can't I be happy right now?" The answer is simple: we have unresolved emotions. So, when we least expect it, the unresolved emotions will reveal themselves from deep within the subconscious mind, robbing us of the ability to be present in the moment. Although it is great to have control over your emotions, if you do not reflect upon the emotion and its root cause, the emotion could cause future problems.

Taking care of your suppressed emotions is actually much easier than most people think. It is as simple as writing down your feelings. Think about the way you interact and converse with people on a daily basis, almost every interaction, if not all of them, are surface-level conversations. "Hey, how are you?" — "I am good, how are you?" We may go a little bit deeper into the things we have done that day, like complain about the job we do not like, but if we are being honest with ourselves, the conversations taking place in society and even among friends and family members hardly ever go beyond surface-level topics. We have a need to express our emotions, and, if we do not, the symptoms of suppression will show up as stress, anxiety, irritability, or anger. Suppression of emotions will also make it difficult to be present in the moment, and so instead of being vulnerable and identifying ourselves with the present moment, we will continue to identify ourselves by the past. Identifying ourselves with the past, and not understanding how to be authentic, is a limited life; it certainly does not resemble freedom.

Is there anything we want to feel in life more than freedom? It is what wars have been fought for; freedom is by far the most important feeling in the world. Unfortunately, it is not a human right; some of us are forced to spend half of our waking hours doing something we do not like or even hate, just to pay the bills. Does that sound like freedom to you? It certainly does not sound like physical freedom, but as we have already mentioned, we always have control over our minds, and so we can always live in a mentally free world. To take full control of your mind, you will have to learn how to be emotionally agile. We live in a world where most people claim to be too busy to simply *be* with their thoughts, emotions, or stories, and this is truly saddening, because ignorance towards compassion, curiosity, and courage is detrimental to the human experience. If you were to tell a man that he would benefit greatly from writing in a journal, he would probably look at you like you were speaking nonsense and reject your advice. This is truly sad and disheartening. Society has conditioned this man and most men to wear a mask that covers up their emotions and authentic self. Men are told to suck it up, be tough, do not cry, push the pain aside and keep on fighting. These are things that we should all do, man or woman, but only in certain situations. If we do not write our feelings down, and we do not have a support system that we can discuss our feelings with, then where and when are we supposed to be with our emotions in a compassionate, curious, and courageous way? It does not matter how tough of a person you are—you will not and cannot function and perform at your best if you do not spend some time to simply be with your thoughts, emotions, and stories.

In what ended up being the last golf tournament Myles played in before an extended time away from the game, he really thought he had a good chance of winning, and so he was excited to play. Just two minutes away from the golf course his car broke down, and so he was in jeopardy of having to withdraw from the tournament. Luckily, due to a frost delay, he was able to make it to the golf course and play. He thought to himself that his car breaking down just minutes from the golf course was going to be added motivation that would help him stay focused on his goal: winning the tournament. Instead, just three holes into the round in which he thought he was excited to be playing, he started to feel strange, and by the time he stood on the fourth tee box he began to experience feelings of boredom, sadness, mental and physical exhaustion and, ultimately, disengagement from the round of golf. The next fifteen holes seemed to take a lifetime, but as he tapped in a short putt to finish his round on the eighteenth hole he felt a flood of emotions rush through his body and chills run down his spine. Myles was aware that these emotions he felt on the golf course were not the emotions he expected to feel that day, and so he took to his journal for the next few days in search of why he felt such negative emotions on the golf course. By putting pen to paper he was able to come to the realization that playing golf was no longer his ultimate purpose, and so he decided to take a four-month break from the game he had once dedicated his entire life to playing. If it were not for emotional agility, Myles would have never been able to spend time with his emotions and become aware of their root cause, which when discovered, allowed him to make a major decision to step away from the game of golf. If he were to have only used emotional intelligence, he would have been aware of the emotions he felt on the golf course, but simply told himself they are of no help in regard to winning a golf tournament, and so he would have continued to wear the mask that portrayed him as a professional golfer and continued working towards a goal that was not true to his authentic self. Emotional agility will always lead you towards your most authentic self; emotional intelligence will lead you towards acting in conformity with social norms.

Most of society is caught in a loop of trying to conform, but the fact is we are all different—we all think, feel, and act differently. It is these differences that make us distinguishable from one another, and it is these differences that make conversations with our fellow humans so interesting. However, when we become caught in the conformity loop, conversations become boring because they are predictable, there is no chance for new ideas to form; this is the way the media and government want us to act. It is a lot easier to control predictable people, but predictability is inherently boring. And boredom is the number one symptom of the ordinarily unconscious person. Do you see that the way you are being told to live is simply a tactic to hold you down? The people in power do not want you to be authentic; they want you to conform. So, it is up to you; suppress your thoughts, emotions, and stories and forever live in conformity, or, express yourself through writing/journaling with compassion, curiosity and courage.

Rx: No longer bottle up feelings and emotions. Spend some time each day writing down how you felt, what was happening that made you feel that way, and why you think you felt that way. Doing this simple task will clear your mind of past baggage that you otherwise will continue to carry with you, thus freeing up space between stimulus and response, which will result in more mindful responses to your external environment.

NEVER BE SATISFIED

"The happiest person is the one who brings forth and practices what is best in himself or herself"

— *Joseph Murphy*

We should always be happy for what we have and what we are working towards but never satisfied, because when we become satisfied with something, we are showing our ignorance to one of the basic laws of the universe: Create or Disintegrate. As much as those of us who are lazy would like to think that we are not getting worse, and that we are just staying the same, that is simply not true. We never stay the same. We are either moving in one direction or another, forwards or backwards. Satisfaction will end in disintegration, as it always leads to complacency. Dissatisfaction is what drives us as humans. Think about this for a moment, if Thomas Edison was not dissatisfied with using candlelight, he never would have created the incandescent light bulb, and we may still be using candlelight to brighten our homes. This is true for many creations; it was dissatisfaction with the way we were doing things that kept the world moving forward. We are not trying to put a negative spin on the word "satisfied," we just want you to become aware that satisfaction breeds complacency, and so in order to keep moving forward, dissatisfaction will keep you driven to create something better.

Dissatisfaction is a built-in motivator; dissatisfaction with life is a healthy state of mind. When we are young, we are taught to be satisfied with what we have, but we disagree with this teaching. We should be grateful for what we have, but never satisfied. We must never mix those two up. Gratitude and satisfaction are completely different things—you can be very grateful and yet still be dissatisfied. Dissatisfaction has given us cars, trains, and planes, and it has taken us out of the cave and into the condominium. Every new invention which has improved your lifestyle and given you greater comfort is the result of someone else being dissatisfied with life as it was. When you become dissatisfied with your life the way it is, you will begin to think of ways to improve it and from there you will set in place a plan to improve your life situation. Usually this plan will involve a list of goals, and these goals should not only improve your life and be fulfilling when accomplished, but also while working towards them. Now, begin to think about how you are living in all aspects of your life, from your position at work and the money you earn to how you treat others in society; how are you living at this moment, compared to how you are capable of living if you rise up to the potential you possess?

Throughout this book, becoming your most authentic self is referred to quite often, and that is because authenticity is one of the two basic human needs aside from the physical requirements of life. We would like to point out that becoming your most authentic self is a goal that in reality is not fully possible. The most authentic version of yourself is always one day in the future; it is always something you will strive to become through growth and self-development. If you become satisfied with who you are, you will stop growing, and, therefore, the process of becoming your most authentic self will slow down and ultimately stop. Never be satisfied with who you are today, because a better, more authentic version of you is waiting just around the corner.

ATTITUDE

Attitude is the composite of our thoughts, feelings, and actions. Our thoughts are on a conscious level, while our feelings are on a subconscious level, and our behavioural pattern is based on our physiology. It is your thoughts, feelings, and actions that when brought together form your attitude. Now, you may be thinking, "Don't actions always follow feelings?" And, the answer is yes, they do. You may also be thinking, "Don't feelings always follow thoughts?" to which the answer is no, not necessarily. You could be saying something positive while feeling something negative, and in this state your mind is conflicted. You must get your thoughts, feelings, and actions all in alignment, so that you feel what most people refer to as inner peace.

With a bad attitude, people will either start to move away from you or you will attract the wrong type of people. With a good attitude, the people you need in your life will gravitate towards you, they will want to get close to you, and they will want to be your friend. Attitude is often the foundation of success or failure; have a positive attitude and you will be fulfilled, have a negative attitude and you will be miserable. Like most things in life, your attitude is a habit, and so you must make it a priority to become aware of your attitude so that you can develop good habits to be able to authentically present yourself as a positive person. A person with a positive and optimistic attitude is always going to get better results than a person with a pessimistic attitude. And a person with a great attitude, well, they are going to get great results. Stop and think throughout the day if your attitude is helping you create the best experience possible at this very moment. If it is not, change it.

GRATITUDE

"The more you are grateful for what you have, the more you will have to be grateful for"

- Zig Ziglar

Saying you are grateful is not the same as feeling gratitude. It is nice to be aware that you should be grateful, but it is a whole different thing to actually feel gratitude. When you feel grateful at the core of your being, you vibrate on such a high frequency that the universe has no choice but to listen. Do not just talk about what you are grateful for, FEEL IT.

Gratitude will make your life more fulfilling in every way. A simple way to start being more grateful is to write down five things you are grateful for when you first wake up in the morning. Before you look at your phone and become distracted by the things you do not have, write down five things that you are grateful for having, or have had, whether they are things, people, or moments. Gratitude can be as simple as feeling grateful for your breath or the chair you are sitting in. Writing the things down that you are grateful for will allow you to become aware of how much you have to appreciate in your life. But, do not forget that writing and saying what you are grateful for is not the same thing as feeling gratitude. Once you have written down what you are grateful for, close your eyes for twenty to thirty seconds and truly feel it at the core of your being.

If you have a job that you do not enjoy, try to find the things about it that are good about it and be grateful for them—remember there is good in everything. Make sure to write these things down and spend a minute or two actually feeling gratitude towards the words you have written. Doing this will help you get through the day with a positive attitude and an increased sense of well-being.

DREAM BIG

If you are already consciously aware of how to get whatever you want, the objective you have chosen is not a worthy goal. You will undoubtedly get it but there will be no growth. The purpose of a goal is to provide an incentive for you to make the necessary changes in your mental and physical conditioning to grow into becoming your authentic self. As you make these changes, what you are doing is raising your level of conscious awareness. This higher consciousness will not just help you achieve your goals—it will increase the fulfillment in your life.

What is the one prerequisite for choosing or setting the right goal? You have to see it and you have to want it. What do we mean by "you have got to see it?" Well, you have an inner eye of understanding. Let us move away from our lower faculties or physical sensory factors that we use so often and instead go inside; as we all have an inner eye of understanding. Do you know that every company you see was once an image in the mind of an individual? As a matter of fact, the book you are reading was just an image in our mind at one time. You must be able to see yourself on the screen of your mind already in possession of the goal, and you must passionately desire it. You do not have to know how you are going to get it, but you must be willing to do anything within your values to get it. We do not care what the goal is you have, if you can see yourself achieving it, and you want it, then you do not need to know how you are going to get it. This may be as cliché as it gets, but... BELIEVE IN YOURSELF!

The mass majority of people are always playing it safe; they never tackle more than they are sure they can handle. These people never invite triumph or disaster, and they never learn the greatness of their mental ability or the strength of their endurance. People who live shallow existences live this way because they are always going after things they are certain they can get. These unfortunate folks are not really living at all, they are simply existing and following someone else's path. On the other end of the spectrum, we have high achievers, people who are potential path finders, eagerly in search of a new trail to blaze. Life is growth and the basic law of your being is "Create or Disintegrate," the choice is yours, simply exist and disintegrate, or live and create.

You may be wondering how to choose a meaningful goal. How do I know what I truly desire? It is a simple answer: You dream. Let your imagination fly, take the lid off your limiting mind and go on a trip, use your marvelous mind to imagine your most authentic desires. In choosing the right goal, we have got to understand that it is absolutely essential that we block out our egoic mind; anything we see that presently exists in our material world should not influence our goals. In other words, shut down the sensory factors, quit looking at the report card, quit looking at the car you are driving, quit looking at the balance sheet; block all that out and turn to your inner mental muscles: reason, memory, will, intuition, perception and imagination. High achievers do not limit themselves, so make sure that your goal is interesting enough that it creates a burning desire inside of you that cannot be put out. There is no reason that you cannot have the vision that you desire. Your imagination is one of your most marvelous mental faculties. Do what all high achievers do and use your imagination properly. Your vision is the promise of what you shall one day be.

"Dreamers are the builders, dream lofty dreams and as you dream so shall you become."

— *James Allan*

We should warn you, every now and then when you are working on your goal and giving it everything you have, you are going to get physically and mentally exhausted, and at these times you will not be exercising a whole lot of wisdom and you may push yourself too hard and go beyond a point you should; this is where failure happens but it is also where growth happens. Napoleon Hill said, *"High achievers never submit to failure."* At any rate, here you are, the risk-taker going after the big win and you failed. Realize this, you will have many losses, some will be devastating, but you will also have many wins. You are never going to find a winner that has not failed. The only time we ever become a failure is when we quit. So make your goal big, make it worth failing for and absolutely refuse to quit.

Do you want to look back at your life when you are older and wonder what your life would have been like if you would had taken risks and chased after your heart's burning desire? Or would you rather be happy for all the risks you took even when you failed because failing taught you a lesson. Understand this, you are not a failure if you fail; you are a failure if you quit. The **First Act In Learning** is to FAIL. The only way you will actually be taking a risk, is by not taking the risk in the first place. An old funeral home owner used to say that it was not the death of the body that upset him; it was the death of all the dreams. It is true that our dreams die with us, and we are the only one that can bring our dreams to reality. Do not be another person who contributes their dreams and aspirations to the richest place on Earth: the graveyard. Put every last bit of effort and passion that you can muster up inside of you into fulfilling your dreams while you still have the chance. By the way... if you are breathing, you still have a chance!

PEACE OF MIND

If you listen to a lot of people, most will tell you that they are interested in things and money, that happiness and peace of mind is their goal. Happiness and peace of mind are not goals, they are conditions of life that all thinking people want and can most certainly attain, but they are not, and should not be, goals. They are the result of a higher degree of both awareness and simple-awareness, which will be yours if you take action in alignment with your values and reflect upon your journey towards your authentic goals. When you give your best effort, with your purpose in mind, you will feel peace of mind and fulfillment.

AFTERWORD

Many of the ideas and practices that are presented in this book will require discipline, hard work, and repetition to make them habits. With that in mind, we would like to remind you that expanding your level of awareness and doing new things that help you to grow is worth it. We would like to take a moment now and ask you, when was the last time you did something for the first time? Was it worth it? From experience, we can tell you that almost everything we have ever done in life that caused us to grow was also worth it, and anything you do for the first time will cause you to grow, so go try something new! As the saying goes, "Most things in life worth having don't come easily," so remember, if it is hard, it is worth it!

We hope that this book has been as life changing for you as it has been for both of us. With current stress and anxiety levels being at an all-time high in the Western world, it is only a matter of time before we see a societal paradigm shift. On a personal level, paradigm shifts happen through repetition and emotional impacts, but on a societal level, the paradigm shift only happens when the evidence becomes overwhelmingly obvious that change is needed. We are quickly approaching that time where it is obvious that change is needed. More and more people are beginning to awaken and realize that the capitalist/industrialist society that we live in is not a meaningful lifestyle. The current way of living among the masses is quite unhealthy, not only physically, but mentally and spiritually as well. The public health data backs this statement up, as there have never been higher percentages of people living with chronic diseases. Together we will make our voices heard; the time for a societal paradigm shift is NOW. The evidence is becoming overwhelming and will soon become so obvious that societies' paradigms will have to shift. Health, authenticity, attachment, and service will soon become the new desires of the average person, as opposed to the current desires of fame, fortune, and power (to be served).

Our goal in writing this book was to:

- Raise your simple-awareness so they you can enjoy life more NOW.
- Raise your awareness so that you can improve your life situation.
- Help you combine the two practices of awareness to live your life in a state of flowing fulfillment.

A HIGHER CONSCIOUSNESS IS DUE TO AN INCREASE IN BOTH AWARENESS AND SIMPLE-AWARENESS. THEREFORE, TO BE MORE AWARE AND SIMPLY-AWARE IS TO INCREASE YOUR LEVEL OF CONSCIOUSNESS.

It is our hope that with our help you have been able to do these things listed above. We also hope that you will continue your journey of self-development towards becoming your authentic self as the world is in dire need of authentic people. Whether you believe it or not, one person can make a huge difference, so never give up on yourself or your vision—the world needs you, and you are the only one that can fulfill the dreams you see in your mind. Work on becoming more aware each day. Think of awareness as your tool kit, the more aware you become, the larger your tool kit will become and the more tools you will be able to carry with you. Awareness will prepare you to be ready to deal with any life situation you find yourself in. Never forget that even when you find yourself in a hard life situation, the situation is not your life and so to clear your mind and gain perspective use your simple-awareness to become present in the moment. In this moment, you will realize that there are no problems; the problems only existed because you had created them in your mind. The combination of simple-awareness and awareness will allow you to write your own story of purpose and fulfillment. Awareness will give you the ability to enjoy life for all it has to offer, during both the good times and the bad. Remember, who knows what is good and what is bad? Perspective is everything, and each one of us has the power to react and respond however we choose, regardless of what happens to us. Decisions, not conditions, determine your destiny. The only question left for you to answer is ARE YOU EVEN AWARE?